EXISTENCE

EXISTENCE

The Mystery of Being

BRUNO VOGT

PARTRIDGE
A Penguin Random House Company

To order additional copies of this book, contact
Toll Free 0800 990 914 (South Africa)
+44 20 3014 3997 (outside South Africa)
orders.africa@partridgepublishing.com

www.partridgepublishing.com/africa

TO MY SON JURGEN
DAUGHTER NADA
AND CLOSE PARTNER RICKY,
THANK YOU FOR YOUR PATIENCE
AND UNDERSTANDING

Contents

PART ONE: MOVEMENTS

PART TWO: PRIMARY FACTORS IN HUMAN EXISTENCE

PART ONE

MOVEMENTS

1

PHYSICAL WORLD UNFOLDING

COSMIC EXPANSION, GROWING ORDER & DEVELOPMENT

In the beginning God created the heavens and the earth (Genesis 1)

How simple it used to be in days gone by! Today, enquiring minds, physicists, astrophysicists, cosmologists, string theorists and other scientists are patiently trying to make sense of the many theories of the beginning (or no-beginning) of our and maybe many other physical worlds.* With question marks hanging around some important incoming scientific information and recent discoveries, such as dark energy and dark matter, some cosmologists fear they will never fully understand the mysteries of our Cosmos.

Yes, towards the end of the twentieth century, leading physicists were beginning to dream of a final theory of the, what they call, Universe. It was aptly named "The Theory of Everything" (TOE). Most notable among them was Stephen Weinberg who unified the electromagnetic and weak nuclear forces in 1967. The idea was to explain all matter, forces as well as space and time with the aim to unify all elementary aspects of the physical world into one single

---

* I have re-named what is known as the universe "Physical World" because in my view the universe proper, "The Whole System of Things", consists of the "Physical World(s)", the "U-Minded World", and the "Primordial World". Now and then I refer to the "Physical World" as "our Physical World" because of the possibility of more than one.

mathematical formula. Well, today, Physicists are still hoping but unexpected obstacles somewhat dampened their enthusiasm.

The most promising means to attain their goal was the String Theory which superseded super gravity as the leading contender for a unified theory. Strings portray the fundamental constituents of nature consisting of one-dimensional vibrating and spinning strands and loops, substituting the familiar and more observation corroborated subatomic particles. Tiny bits of elastic string vibrate and spin in different patterns, each corresponding to a different type of particle whilst specific quantized movements relate to their physical attributes such as mass, charge and spin.

By the mid-1980s, String Theory was refined by incorporating super-symmetry, a mathematical arrangement that unites sub-atomic particles with different values of spin into a common description. However, superstrings (as they were called), needed six additional spatial dimensions, too small to be seen but existing at every point in three dimensional space. Later, different versions of string theory were combined to produce what is known as the heterotic string theory but the complexities of the extra six (hidden) spatial dimensions in terms of geometry and mathematics proved to be extremely challenging. In addition to one-dimensional strings, multi-dimensional membranes (branes for short), working on the same principle as strings, and point like entities were introduced to overcome most of the problems but in the meanwhile the dreams of the 1980's to unify fundamental physics with cosmology took a backseat. Ironically, it was a later version of the all-brane theory, the so called M-Theory developed in 1995 by Edward Witten, a leading pioneer of the string theory and Petr Horava at the Princeton University, U.S.A., that inspired two leading cosmologists, Paul J. Steinhardt and Neil Turok to develop a promising alternative to the generally accepted hot big bang-inflation theory. The model was called the "Cyclic Universe", a new cosmology in which the big bang is not a one-time event but one of many in repeating cycles of physical existence. However, this revolutionary theory (it also accommodates the second law of thermodynamics) could most probably be proved wrong by a recent discovery of gravitational waves caused by the traditional big bang.

Yes, the hot big bang-inflation model has been accepted by scientists and the public alike as the dominant theory of the beginning of space and time for many years (The big bang theory was developed in the early twentieth century and the inflation mechanism was introduced in the 1980's), although no credible explanation is forthcoming on why or how the big bang initially started. Also, notwithstanding the fact that much of the theory agrees with observation, over time many flaws have been detected. Recent discoveries such as dark matter and dark energy were simply added without them having any connection to the existing theory. Then along came the theory of "Eternal cosmic inflation" that led to the possibility of an inflationary multiverse. This idea has been given mathematical form by string theory, however, the marriage of this latest inflationary cosmology to string theory produced a concept I find absurd. How could we realistically live in one of at least 10^{500} physical worlds (universes) in a multi-world (multiverse) in which physical conditions vary from world to world? According to this theory our physical world is an oasis in a landscape of worlds where any physical laws are possible. Surely, nature wouldn't strive for such awkward solution for its existence! Only if scientists find convincing physical evidence would I be converted to support such theory. A limited space big bang-inflation model is more credible than one with an infinitely stretchy space filled with an infinite number of physical worlds.

The big bang must have happened in an extremely contrived manner, very orderly, very precise, not too forceful and not too weak. A too slow expansion would have ended in immediate rapid collapse and a too fast one would have given way to conditions which were not conducive for life to develop. The precision of the big bang reveals itself by the uniform pattern of expansion following the bang. The expansion brought in its wake incredible and extraordinary development. The "Opening-up" of our physical world can be compared to the opening of a flower before full bloom. I fully believe that growing order and natural development is inextricably linked to, and on a parallel course with cosmic expansion. The present distribution of galaxies and galactic clusters is at a constant average density observed in all directions. Even the background heat radiation, said to be a leftover from the energy release of the big bang matter-antimatter annihilation, reveals extremely uniform temperatures in all directions. Nothing detracts from the wonders of existing uniformity, coherence, large scale simplicity, order and harmony of our physical world. Logically, it does not have to be like this. We could very well picture ourselves a world in which arbitrary and haphazard activity abounds, infinite numbers of stars collide, explode, transform, disappear and galaxies that move all over space. Instead we experience an orderly and regimented flow of things and events. Underlying this spatial and temporal order are fundamental constants, physical laws and mathematical rules, in fact the whole physical world seems to be built in accordance to prescribed laws and rules.

Have these rules been structured to serve a purpose? Were they meant to be a means to an end?

The answer is a definite "yes".

The physical laws and mathematical rules are in essence abstract principles that relate to each other in meaningful ways. They ultimately exist for one sole, great purpose:

To ensure optimal existence and continuity thereof …

The laws and rules guarantee a certain consistency from one moment to another. They counteract, at present and for a long time to come, wide spread chaos and general disintegration. These rules guide our physical world to its peak of development and beyond ….

The next step following the establishment of temporal and spatial order and, on a parallel course to the positive influence of cosmic expansion, is the process of natural development, a gradual unfolding or progressive change of nature. In its broader aspect, natural development incorporates growth, the increase in the size of an organism. During the process of natural development, new and improved situations and opportunities emerge which in turn are conducive for further development.

However, natural development does not proceed without interruptions as death and destruction are never far away. "Fierce battles" against degeneration and dissolutions abound. Nevertheless, the inherent factor for success under present circumstances far out-weighs the one for failure, and natural development, not only on our planet, but all over the physical world, will, in favourable conditions, continue unabated.

An important part of natural development on our planet is evolution, the doctrine according to which higher forms of life have gradually arisen from lower forms. The process of change has been toward increased complexity of structure and increased unification and harmonious control of life. However, there are many cases of degeneration, both among plants and among animals, where the usual direction of evolution has been, in a sense, reversed. On the whole, evolution is a unique testimony of how, in nature, in the confines of our planet, the factor for success outweighs the factor for failure.

The following is a concise step by step account of key developments in the history of our physical world. It is imperative to bring these impressive changes and innovations of nature to the fore as it will make people understand how finely tuned cosmic expansion and order paved the way for development and most importantly, how the processes of natural development have collectively contributed to the formation of my concept of "positive and negative phases" in a cycle of physical existence.

As I am a strong believer in a cyclic model (of our physical world), I am hesitant to use the unified theories and the original scheme of inflation to explain the early beginning, especially in lieu of the possibility that the discovery of the so-called dark energy and future results of the large hadron collider at "Cern" Geneva as well as future discoveries in general may still turn physics upside down. However, these theories are still credible and relevant until "proven" otherwise.

Our physical world "saw the light of day" at time X, the first moment of a new cycle.

The physical world re-formation has begun. "Unfortunately", no scientific data is available that could give an insight on activities before time X.

The inflation period, also known as the phase transition, lasted 10^{-32} sec. During this time bubbles of "empty" space began to inflate at an exponential rate, doubling in size every 10^{-34} sec., creating an excited false vacuum with immense negative pressure and incredible "self-created" energy (virtual particles of brief existence). This period was marked by cold and empty conditions and matter and radiation were non-existent. The hyper-inflation ceased with a sudden burst of heat caused by the decay of the false vacuum. The time was 10^{-32} sec. The big bang was in full swing. The physical world, a featureless broth of quantum energy, was now in its most simple state, the condition from which **"things" started to develop.**

Delays in the false vacuum decay rate (quantum fluctuations) created irregularities that most certainly were responsible for the future creation of galaxies and galactic clusters. At 10^{-12} sec., the density was immense and the temperature may have been 1,000,000,000,000,000 ^{0}C. The cosmic material consisted of a fluid of quarks, the first recognisable sub-atomic particles. During this time the unified force (super-force) began to split. First the strong nuclear force separated from the electro-weak force, then the electro-weak force split into the electro-magnetic and the weak nuclear force. At 10^{-6} sec., the quarks have condensed into the more familiar protons and neutrons. At 10^{-3} sec. the particles combined with their anti-particle companions to almost equal proportions. The following annihilation of matter – anti-matter left a residue of matter consisting of protons, electrons, neutrons, neutrinos and photons which in turn prepared the necessary condition for helium synthesis. The remaining anti-particles disappeared inside less than one second.

At 1-sec, the radiation era terminated. The young physical world was filled with electrons, protons, neutrons and neutrinos formed by the photons of the high temperature radiation era. About 3 to 4 minutes after time X and at a temperature of 1,000,000,000 ^{o}C, isotopes of helium nuclei formed by nucleo-synthesis (fusion of protons and neutrons).

At 100,000 years, the background radiation, a result of the matter - antimatter annihilation, had a temperature of 10,000 ^{o}C and the density of matter and radiation were equal.

At approximately 1,000,000 years and at a temperature of 3,000^{o}C atoms have formed and the chemical element hydrogen emerged, the opaque physical system became transparent to light and the background radiation separated from matter.

At 1,000,000,000 years after the big bang, stars, galaxies, clusters and even super clusters of galaxies could be identified.

However, the big bang could not create all chemical elements as the cosmos expanded far too quickly for all necessary reactions to take place. It had just sufficient time to finish off the light elements including hydrogen, helium and lithium. The vast majority of elements vital in the formation of planets like earth and all the life forms found on it were created in another cosmic furnace, a supernova explosion. Such an explosion was the final curtain call for a huge old dying star. This point was reached because it ran out of fuel, became unstable, imploded and the outer layers bounced off its core and blasted into space. All that was left of a gigantic star was scattered debris floating in space. In an ironic twist of fate some of the fossilised debris later became the seed for even greater development within.

Our entire solar system originated from the remains of a dead star. It is called a nebula, a cloud of gas, mainly hydrogen interspersed with particles of cosmic dust. Because of the mutual cosmic attraction of gas molecules and dust particles, the cloud became smaller and denser. Condensation and rotation due to the pressure of starlight exerted over millions of years, created a dense centre, the site of our future sun. Interspersed in the rotating cloud of gas and dust were local centres of condensation which later became our planets. The larger central mass became denser, hotter and soon was hot enough to glow and disperse its own light. The denser it grew the hotter it became until pressure and temperature were sufficient to initiate an atomic reaction by fusing the hydrogen into helium. This increased its source of energy and its glow became intense. A star was born, virtually from the ashes of another star. The inherent power for development seems to be inexhaustible.

Some of the planets may also have been luminous but gradually cooled. The outer planets, because of loss of heat kept their layers of hydrogen compounds but the inner planets, because of their proximity to the sun, stayed hot and in the process lost their surrounding layer of hydrogen atmosphere. They also shrunk in size until only a rocky core was left.

Planet earth evolved between these extremes and experienced optimum conditions for its future development. According to the standard inflationary model, the estimated age of our physical world is 13.8 billion years and our solar system, including earth, is 4.6 billion years.

Our planet is entirely made of matter and we know that in our physical world, matter is the pre-dominant substance and very little anti-matter is to be found. Astronomers put the limit on one part anti-matter in a thousand of all matter.

However, it is a laboratory proven fact that all matter is created with <u>equal amounts</u> of anti-matter (the fact that every particle* is created with a counterpart

---

* Some particles are their own antiparticles, for example the neutrally charged particle of light, the photon.

is a significant contribution to abundant evidence supporting my theory of existence). It is also common scientific knowledge that whenever matter meets anti-matter, they destroy each other in a burst of (neutralised) electro-magnetic radiation. There is apparent proof of this colossal big bang energy release in the observed background radiation that fills the physical world.

If all this is true, why do we exist?

Science tells us that there must have been an early imbalance between matter and anti-matter. It was subsequently calculated that our present physical system derived from a tiny asymmetry of one thousand million and one parts matter to one thousand million parts anti-matter. Equal amounts of matter and anti-matter annihilated each other, leaving this slight residue of ordinary matter that became part of the world we live in.

How could this imbalance between matter and anti-matter occur?

Before science came up with an acceptable explanation, the frequent response was: "it was built into the initial conditions from the beginning!" The way out of ambiguity came in the form of the grand unified theories (GUT).

Imagine a world only 10^{-32} sec. old. It was at that time when the extraordinarily heavy particle X was part of an odd and peculiar melee of densely packed particles. The density was supposed to be 10^{73} Kgm^{-3} and the temperature 10^{28} K. It was theorised that the decay of the X particle brought about ⅔ matter and only ⅓ anti-matter. However, particle X also has an anti-particle, the. On its decay it would produce ⅓ matter and ⅔ anti-matter and thereby keep the overall symmetry. To get out of this "cul de sac", the scientists at first assumed and later demonstrated that there was a fundamental imbalance in the decay rates of particle X and particle. The result was that matter and anti-matter could not completely cancel each other out in this early physical system. The leftover (residue) was what now constitutes our physical world.

Notwithstanding the fact that symmetry is deeprooted in the laws of nature, asymmetry does exist. One of the most prominent examples of symmetry-breaking is the chemical blue print that controls cellular behaviour – DNA. Molecules of DNA have a spiral-shaped geometrical form known as the helix, winding always to the right. All earth life is made from this right handed, spiral-shaped form.

Ultimately, the grand unified theories may not be the answer. One could very well imagine a parallel world to ours consisting of anti-matter, a physical world in which the helix winds to the left. However, it is inconceivable how any mixture of matter and anti-matter initially could ever separate into parallel worlds without first annihilate (neutralising) itself. At the same time one must keep in mind that laboratory experiments and scientific theories may differ from natural events and because symmetry is deeply entrenched in the laws of nature, a parallel anti-matter world would certainly fit well into the overall scheme of things.

At all times, the innate relationship between particles of matter and anti-matter should allude us of the importance of **Polarity in all of nature.**

LIFE

Life is the condition of organized matter that gives organized beings certain powers and functions – in particular the powers of growth and self-reproduction – which are not associated with inorganic matter.

The physical/chemical basis for life is still unknown because the composition of the protoplasm (the elementary material of the living cell) is extremely complex.

The first traces of life, the prokaryotes (bacteria) originated about 3,500,000,000 years ago in what is now Australia and Southern Africa.

How did life come to exist? Was it by chance, complex evolution or some other means?

Biological science hasn't come up with any satisfactory answer so far, but researchers are optimistic that with all the biochemical knowledge and the reasonably well known conditions of the early earth's atmosphere …. and with a bit of luck and lots of patience, they will succeed.

The chemical processes must have started in the early geological era in small and simple ways under optimum conditions but it is my humble opinion that the "sparks" that started it all were of metaphysical origin, a power conjoined to energy (subatomic particles) which I named "Potentia".

The milestone of emerging life is marked by the sudden evolvement of complex biological structures. The composition of a single gene is the result of an enormously complicated process and if one considers that one of the most primitive bacteria, "mycoplasma gallisepticum" contains 170 different genes, one can understand the difficulties scientists have to face. Yet, it did happen and what is even more remarkable, it happened against all the odds.

The prokaryotes could very well have been the beginning and the end of all life on earth. There was no logical reason why there should have been any more development. Evidence suggests that this is what almost happened. Fossils of a more complex life form and next in line, the eukaryotes, were found in rock created almost 2,000,000,000 years later. The power for development must have exhausted itself and was in need of a long rest after its first success!

Thereafter, different lifeforms began to emerge at a greatly increased rate. The development, or more appropriately, the evolution of plants and animals was now in full swing.

Evolution is a term used to describe the natural process of slow transformation by which an organised being or system of things, after persisting for a while, gives rise to another, usually of increased complexity of structure, unification and harmonious control of life.

Yet, there are many cases of degeneration among animals and plants where increased complexity was unsuitable and a return to a simpler form was more advantageous.

It must be clearly stated that the theory of evolution does not as yet stand on a perfectly secure base and it is erroneous to speak of the doctrine as fully demonstrated. On the other hand corroborating evidence for evolution has now come from many scientific sources such as palaeontology, comparative anatomy, embryology and bio chemistry. The theory is widely accepted among scientists and ordinary people, but a lot of work still has to be done to refine it.

One of the more controversial and therefore more well known factors in the evolution process is the theory of natural selection – the survival of the fittest. It is based on the (in some cases verified) assumption that in the struggle for existence, unfit (relative to circumstances and the environment in which they live) plants, animals and in lesser instances, humans, are naturally eliminated. The struggle may be between a living creature and inanimate nature, between one race of animal and another, between rival males and so forth.

To understand and to acknowledge evolution and the theory of natural selection we ought to recognise the role of "random alterations" (mutations) in the DNA of living cells. They provide the variations and different attributes to all things alive. It must be noted that only a small minority of mutations among the many produced account for an improvement in the abilities of the host organism. Successful mutations enable an organism to survive in changing environmental conditions. In animals and later in humans they were responsible for brain development which in turn led to more sophisticated hunting skills and countless other advantages. It culminated in the human's present domination but also the wanton destruction of fauna and flora, indeed a very forceful demonstration of the adage "survival of the fittest".

Evolution is a reasonable interpretation of organic nature, however, the theory of natural selection and the originative and isolation factors gave rise to many unanswered questions.

Natural development in biology refers primarily to the growth of plants, animals and humans. It is worth mentioning because unlike evolution, we are direct witnesses to this type of development within evolution. To be able to watch a beautifully coloured caterpillar emerge from a simple fertilized egg cell, and then transform itself into a cocoon out of which an even more beautiful butterfly greets the rising sun, is truly a marvellous experience. Nature is filled to the brim with similar examples but again, as with evolution, many questions regarding natural growth (of an organism) remain unanswered.

SPEARHEAD OF EVOLUTION

Undoubtedly, humankind is the Spearhead of evolution. We can illustrate this by contracting the earth's lifespan of approximately 4.6 billion years into one year. Earth was born on the first day of January. The first traces of life emerged already at the end of February. After this, a huge gap developed and the next, more complex life form was found at the end of October. Exactly why it took so long for the Eukaryotes to make an appearance is still a scientific mystery. Leaving this momentous event behind, evolutionary development began to accelerate at an ever increasing rate. Chordates originated on November 17, the vertebrates on November 21, mammals on December 12, primates on December 26, anthropoids on December 30 at 1-00 am, hominids on December 31 at 10-00 am and finally homo sapiens on December 31 at 11-56.5 pm.

The behaviour pattern of animals in the early part of this sequence is mostly stereotyped. Later, the pattern becomes richer until we reach homo sapiens where complex actions predominate. The correlation between behaviour and brain is exemplified in the development of a particular brain region coinciding with a modification of response or behaviour pattern. By "chance" mutation and selection, some of the lowly creatures of the past developed over time a type of automatic switch-board, the central nervous system situated in the spinal cord and ending in the brain. With great certainty can we state that today's sophisticated nervous system, comprising the central and peripheral system, originated from primitive response reflex systems of animals lower down the ladder of development. In human reflex action, the stimulated nerve carries a message to the spinal cord and brain from where it is transmitted back to produce the response to the affected organ. Voluntary action originates in the motor cortex of the brain which is further divided into specialized sections that control specific muscles. Messages travel from here to the spinal cord and via nervous processes to the muscles. In nervous action several activities are involved. Firstly, the message (pain for example) goes to the brain via the spinal cord where the position of the pain and circumstances are analysed. It then decides to act for the pain to stop. A message is sent back down from the motor cortex to the spinal cord and out to the muscles of the arm or hand to take action. There are various combinations of actions, for example voluntary, nervous activity which is learned or conditioned. Many reflex actions are also learned and are called conditioned reflexes.

The evolution of mind proceeded on a parallel course with the evolution of the brain. Brain development does not mean that the creature with largest brainsize possesses the most developed brain. The brain of a dolphin is approximately the same size as ours but it lacks complexity. The largest size human brain ever recorded belonged to a mentally handicapped person. Nevertheless, on average the human brain has doubled in size over the last two million years.

The brain consists of three parts, the brainstem, the mid-brain and the fore-brain (cerebrum). The brainstem is the most primitive and the mid-brain the more complex part, but it is the fore-brain that appears to have grown most with evolution. It is also thought to be the "the seat of the mind", although nobody so far has found any evidence.

To get a clearer image of brain development, let us look at the brain of a fish, a dog and a human.

The fish, a creature well adapted to its natural habitat but slightly left behind in the gradual un-folding of nature, possesses a brain that is not more than a tiny bulge at the end of the spinal cord. It consists of a brainstem, mid-brain and a minute cerebrum. The brain's primary function is the body's autocontrol. It may have marginal consciousness, however, it lacks any semblance of consciousness as we know it.

A dog is highly conscious. Its cerebrum is large and developed to serve its self-governing functions. By comparison to fish and reptiles, the first mammals in the history of evolution needed millions of additional braincells to accommodate all the visual, auditory, olfactory and tactile data required for their fight for survival, their modified feeding habits and their obligation to provide food, care, warmth and education to their offspring. Increased development generates more flexibility and freedom but also demands more discipline. Their advanced brain power may even have produced the very first signs of emotions such as love, compassion and concern.

The greater part of the human brain is taken up by the cerebrum, the organ of thought and the seat of the faculties that made homo sapiens different and vastly superior in specific areas to animals. The cerebrum is the dome shaped mass at the top of the scull. It is divided into two halves and covered with wrinkles not unlike the surface of a wall nut. The total of the human intellect, memory and reason is accounted for in the grey matter of the cerebrum. The underlying white matter contains nerve fibre tracts that associate with areas of the cerebral cortex. The wrinkles of the cerebral cortices increased the cortical surface area. This innovation was the main cause of the human brain's greater development potential over the dolphin's brain of similar size.

Human brains have evolved in such a way as to take into account the dual aspect of nature, the unity of the universe and the interrelationship of its parts. One of the two quite distinct brain hemispheres specialises in holism and the other in reductionism, one directly contributing to the mystical and the arts, the other to the rational mind and the combination of the two to general survival and development. The operation of both mental modes is essential for balanced human consciousness.

The human brain is still the ultimate computer with its tens of billions of primitive processors, the nervecells (neurons), signalling to each other by means of electrical impulses. For example, a positive signal is activated and sent to the next cell only if it exceeds a relative critical limit. The nervecell then makes a decision either to act positively and carry on the message (excitatory action) or act negatively and reduce the next cell's electrical activity (inhibitory action). The reduction in electrical activity is done by the release of a chemical substance into the narrow gap between the nerve cell end and the next cell (the nerve cell ends can be artificially influenced by the intake of drugs that give rise to mood, perception and behaviour changes such as depression and hallucinations).

Sensory processing, memory and planning are important programmes of the brain, however, it is mind and self-consciousness that sets humans apart from animals.

To our knowledge, the greatest step forward in the development of our physical world, is the evolution of the human mind.

HUMAN MIND

The universe is realised ….. by a tiny, abstract existent entity, a space-time bound, still extremely primitive replica of the U-Mind (Universal Mind).

Brain evolved from primeval matter, however, mind evolved by means of the power of the brain. It is an invisible tool enabling humans to survive, develop, create and, on a higher level of thinking, establish and develop a conscious connection to, and understanding of the U-Mind. What is mind? What is the human mind? What is this mysterious, complex "Thing" that stands at the forefront in the development of our physical world.? Is it a tangible part of physical nature?

Questions, Questions, Questions ….

At present it is many "things" to many people; one's inclination, direction of will, state of thought and feeling, intellect or "that" which thinks, knows, feels and wills. It may also be defined as "something" that combines parts, or all of the above.

Over centuries philosophers have voiced their opinion on the subject of mind. Their views range from the extreme materialistic denial of mind to the moderate materialistic view where mind is an epiphenomenon of physical brain activity. Others went one step further and took the platonic dualistic approach where the human possesses an independent mind, connected to the body. Interactionism in this case means the body acts upon the mind and vice versa. The double aspect theory is a view that there is only one kind of substance and body and mind are two aspects of this substance.

Let us try to analyse the mystery of mind.

There is no known physical location of mind. This is the conclusion after long and intensive scientific research into the brain and nervous system. Neuroscientists still have yet to come across a physical organ inside the brain that would bear any resemblance to what the majority of humans would define as "mind". There are no signs that point to it being a physical object or something of organic nature, but with the entire mental content of conscious experience as evidence for its existence, it is very difficult to consider and even more difficult to conclude that mind may be just an abstract concept, albeit of great complexity.

Mind or the mind plays such an important part in the lives of humans that many wrongfully refer to it as something with objective reality. It is almost universally accepted as being the seat of our intellect, feelings and will. This manifestation came about by the apparent necessity to conveniently accommodate in one system all rational and abstract thoughtprocesses and their results, deliberations as well as new ideas and notions together with their inevitable effects of feelings and emotions that ultimately provide incentive and motivation (or the opposite) and, lastly, the power of choosing or determining (free will). The power of mind in shaping one's destiny is well documented.

Is mind just an abstract concept or is there more to it?

To become more familiar with its "nature" it is important to know more of the inner workings of our brain and incoming sensory activity. We must realise that what we see, feel and hear is not what actually happens outside ourselves, beyond our senses. On-going experiences are familiar projected images, familiar sounds, smells, tastes and touches but they are only the results of in the brain processed information that were received from the outside in the form of vibrations of different frequencies, all part of the energy scheme of our physical world. Very low frequencies for hearing and touch, higher frequencies for heat and higher still for vision. Perception of colour is the result of the variation of wavelengths in light. Incoming radiation undergoes pre-sorting and processing in particular organs such as the retina or cochlea for example. Electrical signals in the form of positive electrical waves (impulses) are then sent from nerve cells along their axions via the thalamus into the cortex. Neuroscientists regard parts of the thalamus, the nucleus reticularis thalami (a network of cells covering the front and sides of the thalamus) as the information controlling access and exit gate to and from the cortex. It may well be the key organ to explain consciousness (awareness) and consciousness is said to be the waking state of mind. However, mind itself is extremely elusive!

Memory is the ability of retaining and reproducing mental, emotional or sensory impressions. The hippocampus serves as a conscious memory processing facility although various regions nearby are storage areas for sub and unconscious memories. The magic word in memory is Impression. The greater the Impression, the more efficient is memory.

Just how much we lack understanding of the inner workings of the brain and how much we still have to learn and discover is shown by the fact that neuroscientists, besides electrical activity and the chemical involvement in activity-changes, know very little of, for example, the coding of impressions nor the mode of action in the recall of memory. Even if we could reasonably understand the function of memory, it would only represent a small step toward an overall understanding of the complex integrated system of the brain and an intimate knowledge of this system is all important because:

> It is the whole of the brain with most of the functions of all utilised areas working in combination that causes one powerful packaged mental effect. It is this effect that we generally refer to as **Mind.**

The process involves complex interactions between incoming sensory activity, on-going conscious and, to a lesser extent, subconscious experiences (for example, dreams etc.), recalled memories (including past emotional experiences) and still exerting a powerful influence, past experiences deeply impressed in the unconscious, for example penetrating suggestions and systematic indoctrinations. From the many and complex interactions, the principal interactions are the comparisons between input data and activated (or re-activated) memory data of past experiences. These comparisons lead to re-evaluations that may result either in a (mental) conflict situation or, as in most instances, "winner takes all". Deeply stored past emotional experiences most certainly influence drive and decision making. The "packaged" overall effect of this global brain activity is:

> For every moment a new, but in most instances little changed inner mental content turned into a specific model of the external and internal world:

The (abstract*) concept of mind.**

Notwithstanding the fact that mind is not organic and has no known location inside the brain, the mind of an individual human being can still be regarded as to be an entity***, albeit abstract. The general criteria for anything abstract-conceptual to be considered an abstract entity are the following:

a) The concept has to be inferred by means of abstract reasoning, if possible substantiated by mathematical evidence or measurements, but logically cannot include abstract concepts such as "Power" or "Capacity".
b) The concept ought to possess specific identity and quality.
c) The concept has to be useful for some purpose, potentially acceptable and successful in its use.
d) The concept cannot be part of any traditional system of belief (religion).

Individual human and developed animal minds fulfil all the above criteria. The individual human mind possesses a specific identity, quality and characteristic by virtue of specific evolutionary brain-mind development, social, cultural and

---

*   Separated by the operation of the mind, as in forming a general concept from consideration of particular instances.

**   A human being possesses only one mind. There is no second or third mind.
       With a sense of disbelief I read in a recent bestselling book on the subject of the power of mind that we possess within us a second mind, a subconscious mind. The author or his source(s) may have erroneously designated normal brain activities in the subconscious and unconscious as that of a second mind. In my view, the subconscious is the initial storeroom of memory where daily mental experiences are recorded. Some impressions stay for days or longer, others fade away almost immediately, all depending on the depth of impression. Some exceptional experiences "dig themselves" deeply into the unconscious, the basement store of memory, where they linger for a lifetime. The most common and most impressive among them are either extraordinary happy experiences on one end of the scale or deeply sad and shocking experiences on the other end. But another type and of particular interest to us is the gradual and sometimes systematic planting of an idea or ideas into the unconscious by means of repetitive suggestions/autosuggestion. These experiences (e.g. of a parenting, religious, ideological or personal nature), strongly affect your mind and subsequently your whole being in either positive or negative ways (for more information see "Mind Power").

***   Entity: being, existence, from latin entitas, - atis – ens. Ens rationis: An entity of reason, existing purely in the mind (which I emphasise with the word "abstract").

environmental influences, genetic propensities and dispositions. On a general scale of values the quality of human minds range from highly intellectual, dynamic-balanced and creative on one end of the scale, to extremely "sick", unstable and destructive on the other end.

The initial process of a <u>growing mind</u> is analogous to building a jig-saw puzzle whereby we assemble within a framework, by learning and by trial and error, different pieces, each one relating to the other in a more or less meaningful way until we gradually become aware of an image of the world we live in. By adding more pieces, the image becomes clearer, bigger and better or ... worse.

"It" emerges, arises and evolves.

HUMAN MIND & REALITY

Why do the majority of humans ignorantly imbue mind with concrete existence, with reality?

Yes, most people use the term "Mind" on a daily basis without discretion or discern. For many it is inconceivable that the human mind is not an organic part of the brain. Unfortunately, most people don't really care as they are occupied with the challenges of everyday living. However, the ones that are interested in the mysteries of body and mind are astutely aware of a wide chasm that exists between reality-related brain activity and its effects such as thoughts, ideas and …. Mind.

The gap between the real world and the mental world began to exist ever since humankind engaged the faculty of reasoning. But is the gap really as wide as we think it is? We are inclined to think so because of our familiarity with the external world and relative ignorance of our inner, mental world. The answer to the following question may significantly narrow the perceived gap between the two worlds.

What is reality?

Again, as with the search for an answer to the question "What is mind?", philosophers have been debating this milestone question for thousands of years without ever reaching agreement or a common understanding as to the inherent nature of reality. Even to this day, the reality of a simple solid object, the likes of a chair for example, is still a matter of contention. Some contemporary natural philosophers maintain that objects of any kind are just forms of matter acting as data transmitters that send vibrations of different frequencies to our senses (data receivers). The senses in turn send pre-processed signals by means of electromagnetic impulses to the brain for final processing. It is only in our mind that objects are finally recognised for what they are. These protagonists infer that objects of any kind is matter in various forms and therefore part of the energy scheme of our physical world. Objects have no independent reality of their own because **the Mind is the "birthplace" of reality;** without the mind's intervention, everything simply

—IS—

I fully endorse and wholeheartedly agree with this view, however, for practical reasons insist on the continued use of the human invented term "reality".

To avoid the possibility of ending up in a quagmire of incomprehensible theories, we ought to be guided by the conventional meaning of the term:

Reality is the state or fact of being real, that which <u>actually exists</u>, not that which is imaginary, illusory, virtual, abstract or assumed.

However, because of recent advances in physical sciences and natural philosophies, current and future "realities" ought to be <u>categorised</u> to suit new, specific and unconventional fields of knowledge.

Now, guided by the conventional meaning of the term "reality", the great divide between the physical/biological reality of the brain and its functions, and the abstract concept of mind, seems to be as pronounced as ever. Yes, in everyday life, for the purpose of our own survival, there has to be a distinct divide between the world of reality and the mental universe. On the one side of the divide we perceive concrete existence and on the other side a composite of many worlds: illusions, fantasy, dreams and imaginations share the territory with normal inferential patterns of thought as well as abstract, inferentially structured thoughts, ideas, concepts, theories and conclusions that manifest in principles, rules and laws as found, though distinctly separated, in philosophy, psychology, physics, economics, politics and mathematics. Among the innumerable concepts found in all fields of abstract thought, **a few stand out as if they are part of reality.**

These concepts seem to occupy the middle ground between reality and idea.

They exist, not objectively, but in every other aspect. The arguably most well-known is "mind". The term is widely used in our lives whilst in psychiatry and psychology (psyche) the mind takes centre stage. Its appeal and usefulness is universal.

The brain is generally perceived to be the organ or "workshop" of mind, however, **where does the physical/biological reality end and the mental/abstract begin?**

Does the brain itself incorporate the end of reality and the beginning of the abstract? Unfortunately, progress in neuroscience and research into the mental aspects of humans is still lagging behind the research developments of most material sciences and technology. Understandably, the restrictions imposed by the limited access to the live human body is the main reason for the relative slow progress. I am hopeful that sometime in the near future collaborating teams of neuroscientists and psychologists will be able to solve some of the outstanding mysteries of brain processing, such as impression coding, memory recall and the global network that ultimately effects mind.

Mind and consciousness is not a human prerogative. In higher developed animals a kind of lower level mind/consciousness replaced some of the natural impulses by which primitive animals are guided. The divide between the reality of the brain and the mental world seems to have arisen with the demise of instinct and sense related perception and the simultaneous rise of conscious thought and rational understanding.

In conclusion: The individual, self-conscious human mind cannot be seen nor pinpointed inside or outside the brain because it is not organic and not part of reality but it is also not just an idea because the term "idea" covers a wide field that includes fiction and fantasy. However, it is an entity that exists in an abstract, non-actual, non-conventional way, making its presence felt in every sphere of human life. The great scientific and technological achievements, the advances in the human sciences, the genius displayed in art and literature as well as our improving humanitarianism bear testimony to its abstract existence.

Yes, the individual human mind is an abstract existent entity, a mental package of one's internal and external world created from the mental content of present and past brain processed experiences. Its identity, quality and characteristics is determined by the quality and type of "mental intake", specific evolutionary brain/mind development, genetic propensities and dispositions as well as social, cultural and environmental influences. In short, the human mind is *an Epiphenomenon of (past & present) physical brain activity,*

and in simple words:

a mental Package of how I see, feel and understand the inner and the outside world.

The mind determines, to a very large extent, our life's direction and almost entirely, the way we behave, think, feel and view the world we live in.

The divide between physical reality and what is conceived to be "mental abstract" will remain with us for a long time. Nevertheless, sometime in the future (with greater knowledge at our disposal), what I now understand to be "mind" may be viewed in a different light. "Mind" may consequently be re-analysed, re-evaluated, re-classified and even re-named.

Creating a mechanical mind is a scientist's dream. However, without an emotion-charged super complex (human like) memory, memory recall, comparison and evaluating system etc., the efforts of trying to make this dream a reality may just yield another robot-mind. I feel it is more important trying to build a bridge across the divide by improving our knowledge in neuroscience and psychology followed by intensive interaction between these and other fields of science.

As an abstract concept, "Mind" stands supreme, however, it is not the only concept of significance and great appeal. Notable examples are to be found in physics. Just consider the usefulness of concepts such as "gauge symmetry" and "fields" in quantum theory, "strings" and "membranes" in string theory and even "particles" in quantum theory. Many more are sure to follow, but the one that towers above all the others in terms of usefulness, successfulness, appeal and …. controversy is "Energy".

"Energy is the capacity of a material body, system of bodies or of radiation to do work", in the sense the term is used in physics. It exists as concept and is utilised in many different forms and can be transformed from one form to another but never created nor destroyed.

The concept of energy found its way into science as an abstract idea and to this day, physicists will not commit themselves to explain the inner nature and/or the origin of energy. For them it is sufficient to know that it exists (as concept only).

Yes, energy may be a concept, but in the sense the term is used in physics, it is enormously helpful and practical, the very reason it has become so well established. This success permeated through to the general public. They saw no reason why the definition of energy (the capacity of a material body, system of bodies or of radiation to do work) should be limited "to do work" only. Why not extend it and replace it with "to produce an effect"? Surely, the release of an immense amount of energy after dropping an atomic bomb for example, had nothing to do with "work done"? However, this kind of thinking is not in line with physics definition of energy which relates only to its application and not its universality. Nevertheless, the general public still embraced the term but in many instances, its familiarity has turned the abstract concept into something real, solid. Even Einstein once remarked analogically that matter is nothing but frozen energy!

"Energy" and "Mind" certainly exist, not in reality but as abstract concepts. In addition, the mind of an individual can also be regarded as to be an "abstract existent entity", but the same cannot be said of "energy". The term is related to "power", "content" and "ability" and therefore cannot be considered to be an entity.

Scientific research has now entered the stage where certain phenomena and mathematical constructs, concepts and entities are increasingly going to play prominent roles. To avoid confusion and misrepresentations in the future regards their reality and existence, it is imperative that we create new levels of existence in addition to our reality.

LEVELS OF EXISTENCE

It is unquestionably important to reduce confusion regards the ambiguity of "things existing". Basically, we have to differentiate between a "thing" that is real (actually and factually existing), a "thing" that exists in the mind only and a "thing", entity or concept that truly exists, not in reality or fact but as abstract entity or/and concept. For this reason I would like to take the opportunity to introduce a new level of existence (Level C), an inferred, formed by the human mind imaginary extension to reality and "home" to entities and concepts that cannot but exist, embody magnitude, value, usefulness and appeal:

"Abstract Existence" or
"The Abstract State of Being".

This level of existence is not a fragment of the imagination but occupies the peculiar and strange middle-ground between reality and idea, and most importantly, it exists. Anything categorised as to be **"abstract existent,"** exists as an entity or concept in a manner that is unconventional, unreal and nonfactual-abstract, but it ought to be emphasized that it is more than a simple abstraction and more than something existing in idea only.

In this context, the previously discussed concept of "mind" ought to be classified as to be an "Abstract-existent Concept" and the individual mind of a human or "higher" animal can be regarded to be an "Abstract-existent Entity".

Developments in psychology, philosophy, theoretical physics and other sciences will, inevitably, necessitate the use of such level of existence. Its introduction should clarify misunderstandings and misinterpretations regards the pseudo-reality of new and existing concepts.

To avoid or at least to reduce the ambiguity of "things" in the order of existence, I would also like to take the opportunity to introduce an initiatory classification of different "Levels of Existence" and, embracing the notion that reality itself is a concept rather than believe in an independent reality of things, allows me to "fine tune" the meaning of reality to suit new circumstances in our changing world. In our quest to push the frontiers of knowledge and science further and further back into the unknown, we have encountered increasing uncertainty and vagueness of what constitutes reality, especially in the strange world of quantum mechanics and particle physics. We have also discovered a vastly changed reality to the one we are used to in physical implications of Einstein's theories of relativity.

EXISTENCE LEVEL "A": REALITY, CLASS I

This is the conventional reality of our familiar world. It conforms entirely to classical laws of science, logic and reason but excludes the mental universe, e.g. thoughts, ideas and the abstract.

REALITY, CLASS II:

This encompasses all extreme physical implications of the special and general theories of relativity and associated fields. The nature of reality, Class II differs considerably from the one on which Newtonian physics is based (Class I).

REALITY, CLASS III:

The micro world of atoms and molecules (common sense ideas about the nature of matter are starting to break down).

REALITY, CLASS IV:

The weird world of subatomic phenomena as structured by quantum physics and <u>verified by experimental observation</u> e.g. subatomic particles as observed on photographic plates as first traces of physical reality. In terms of scale, the difference between the atomic level and the subatomic level is as great as the difference between the atomic level and our familiar world. To actually see the nucleus (the size of a grain of salt), the atom would have to be the size of a fourteen storey building and the electrons orbiting the nucleus would be the size of dust particles.

EXISTENCE LEVEL "B": THE MENTAL WORLD OF HOMO SAPIENS

It encompasses all human thoughts, ideas, notions, concepts, images, visions, dreams, phantasies, illusions, delusions and hallucinations, as well as rational awareness of feelings, e.g. pleasure, pain, happiness and desire. Also included are diverse sciences of mind, psychiatry, psychopathology etc. etc.

Mental products of the human mind are space-time bound, however, a link exists to existence level "X" and the U-Mind, as evidenced by the existence of a parallel creative (and destructive!) human mind and the human's natural grasp of the language of nature: Mathematics.

EXISTENCE LEVEL "C": ABSTRACT EXISTENCE

Thrust beyond all classes of reality, existence level "C" occupies the strange middle ground between reality and idea. It accommodates concepts and entities that embody value, usefulness, appeal and exist in a non-actual, non-conventional way. They are more than simple abstractions and are not to be compared to and confused with realities, real "things" and/or with "things" existing in the mind only. Existence Level "C" bridges the seemingly enormous divide between our so-called reality and our mental world (both immersed in ordinary space-time) as well as the gigantic divide between the above mentioned worlds and levels of existence beyond ordinary space time.

Suggested Classification:

Abstract Existence, Class I: Psychology and associated sciences, for example "mind" (Concept and Entity).

Abstract Existence, Class II: Physics and associated sciences, for example, subatomic particles in their unobserved raw state (Concept and Entity); Energy (Concept); Power (Concept); etc.

Additional classes can be allocated as and when needed.

EXISTENCE LEVEL "X": The U-Minded World

Inferred by the writer, this is a world of paradox, a world still beyond our comprehension, a world not immersed in ordinary space-time but in wholeness, controlled by the Universal Mind (U-Mind).

Devoid of physical movement-energy, the U-Minded world's powerful counterpart is "Potentia" (or U-Minded Motion-Power). "Potentia" cannot not exist. It is the "subjective" prerequisite and source of all reality, ideas, thoughts, abstract concepts and entities. It is also the "subjective" source of the stunning beauty and incredible diversity of nature on our planet. I perceive the wholeness of the U-Minded world to be unbroken U-Minded existence, devoid of fragmentation and ordinary space-time as we know it. In the top layer of this level of existence, the U-Mind "invented" the laws and rules of nature, "implanted" in "Potentia".

EXISTENCE LEVEL "Y": The Primordial World

The Triad, the symbol of the primordial world, reflects the inner nature of the universe, and, yes, the primordial world is still with us, but on Level "Y"; a timeless reminder of why we are here.

In the realm of existence, "the Absolute" does not exist (and outside existence is "Non-existence", which cannot exist!) because the Absolute is split (in the primordial world) into two different primordial entributes, "Pos" and "Neg", opposing each other but still trying to re-unite, however, prevented from doing so by the third primordial entribute "Neut", situated between them.

This, in descriptive language, is the "principle of existence" and "primary cause". Its effect is "Agitation" resulting in "reasonably balanced" interaction between Pos, Neut and Neg, all thanks to an "awakening" primordial mind, set on balanced existence.

LEVEL Z: The Absolute

"The Uncaused self, independent of relation to other things". In the realm of existence, the absolute does not exist. It is simply an idea.

The introduction of these levels of existence, in particular reality levels Class I to IV, has become a priority to try to reduce confusion regards the unconventional reality of entities and forms, localities and attributes of "things" discovered during the later stages of scientific research.

Mysteries abound, new dimensions have to be added to our familiar three spatial dimensions to make theories "work". The new physics, especially quantum mechanics and particle research lead the way in acknowledging and accepting phenomena that used to be the prerogative of mystics and philosophers. Notions, the likes of "Massless Particles" that are unlike particles of dust but rather "Tendencies to exist" belong to the very outer edges and beyond an already extended reality. But whatever the form or property of these particles of matter and radiation may be, and whatever our perceptions concerning their behaviour are, **they exist.**

The pertinent question is: what is the measure of their objectivity, or how tangible is their existence? We know they are not pure figments of the imagination, nor are they free creations of the mind and above all, they are not material objects either. However, a subatomic particle's actual existence is uniquely determined during experiments by its interaction with an "observing system"; for example, the system consists of an experimental set-up that includes an observation and measuring device but most importantly, it also includes the human mind to analyse the results. The evidence of the elusive moving particle's <u>actual existence</u> is in the form of a physical effect, for example specific individual traces for each particle type, on a photographic plate. Particles thus "brought into being" and manipulated in bubble-chamber physics, emulsion (photographic plate) physics and counter physics are first signs of physical reality, however, because of their fringe status, I categorised them as belonging to the, presently, bottom class of existence Level "A": Reality Class IV (classified as Group 1 particles). However, a particle in its raw, natural state (classified as Group 2 particle, Type B) and one in its raw state during an experiment <u>before</u> an experimental observation is done (classified as Group 2 particle, Type A), **is steeped in total uncertainty.**

There is no proof of its actual existence, no actual sign of its identity, its "structure" its whereabouts and its motion at any given time. From a scientist's point of view, raw state particles are more like manifestations of interacting fields. The scientist's knowledge of a raw-state particle is purely theoretical. He knows "it" exists and he can guess its approximate location, however, he cannot pinpoint it at any given time. What he also knows is that concentrations of myriads of these ghostly entities make up matter and radiation or more specifically, "tables and chairs, sunlight and air!" The "non-reality" of a raw-state particle is simply baffling. The only logical alternative I have under these circumstances is to classify the two types of raw-state particles as to be **abstract existent entities** belonging to existence Level "C", the middle ground between reality and idea.

How real is light (Electromagnetic radiation) we may ask. The answer to this question is determined by what is meant by "light". Visible light as we experience it in our daily lives is obviously part of our reality (Level "A", Class I), but how real are the properties of a beam of light?

The pioneers of modern physics have discovered and experimentally confirmed that a beam of light has a dual "personality", it has either a strange wave or a particle like behaviour pattern. However, the dual nature of light manifests itself separately in interactions depending upon the choice of scientific experiment or specific application.

I have already classified particles of matter and electromagnetic radiation (includes visible light) into two distinct categories, the existence Level "A," Reality Class IV particles and the two types of abstract existent, existence Level "C", Class II raw state particles.

The particle of light is named photon and the physicists responsible for its discovery are Max Plank and Albert Einstein. It won them both a Nobel prize (in 1918 and 1921 respectively) for laying the foundations of quantum physics.

For practical reasons we state that the wave and particle-like behaviour are known properties of light, the truth is, they are not. They are only properties of our interaction with light. Limited human perception and understanding prevents us to grasp the actual underlying properties of light. It would be more appropriate to say that light presents itself to us either wave or particlelike in specific interactions. This still leaves us with the question: "where does the light wave fit into our scheme"? The answer is short and simple: nobody knows for certain. All we know is that light waves are always associated with groups of particles, for example when a beam of light passes through a screen with two parallel slits onto a photographic plate, it effects an interference pattern on the film that could only materialise if the light behaved like a wave. If the intensity of light is turned down considerably, individual spots (demonstrating its particlelike behaviour) appear on the film. These spots slowly build up to reveal the same pattern as before. The wave particle duality comes into sharp focus if the light source is manipulated in such a way that it sends only one particle (photon) at a time. Its effects on the film is like that caused by a mini-minute version of meteor as it enters the atmosphere: the photon burns up in a speck of brilliance. Yet, dot by dot, the same interference pattern emerges; It seems as if the unseen, shrouded in mystery raw state particle is still part of a slow motion wave while in flight. This example highlights the reason why I located the unobserved raw state particle to existence Level "C" and classified it as an abstract existent entity. There is no scientific proof (as yet!) of its particularised existence. The same can be said of other sub-atomic particles as they also display wavelike behaviour in their raw state whilst in motion. The wave and particle characteristics of light/radiation and of matter are unified by quantum mechanics in a unique mathematical "entity", the "wave function". It is the quantum physicist's description of the nature of a particle before an experimental observation or measurement is done. According to the "Copenhagen interpretation of quantum mechanics", the raw-state particle in motion does not exist as such at any place or in any discrete material form at all. It exists only in the way the wave function describes it and the wave function suggests that it only exists as an "endlessly proliferating number of possibilities" (as a development or evolvement of possibilities in time). In contrast, matter particles in their raw, natural state, making up an atom of any chemical element are <u>forced</u> (in the truest sense of the word) to exist (in harnessed motion) within a specified space according to rules and laws of physics. In such state the raw particles still do not exist at any one place or in any discrete material form at all. It is important to recognise that even under normal, forced conditions, inherent uncertainty and potentiality remain. Until a more profound theory takes its place, I recognise and accept the "Copenhagen interpretation" as an important guideline to my own views of the abstract qualities of raw-state particles.

In conclusion: The dynamic raw-state particles of matter and radiation exist in abstract mode on existence Level "C" until their exact moment of change by way of experimental observation or measurement by experts (which brings them into so-called reality on existence Level "A", Class IV). The physicist's jargon for such momentous change is "Quantum Jump", transition or in reference to the wave function, "wave function collapse".

Some people may be bewildered by my inclusion of Class II to Class IV reality, but I justify their inclusion due to the fact that conditions of their reality are very unlike our familiar conditions and circumstances. Class II reality is the physical "playground" conditioned by the theories of relativity. Not only are the physical results extremely puzzling to a lay person, they are also in conflict with our normal perceptions of common sense reality. Space and time have ceased to be separate. In the realm of super high velocities, incredible changes occur to people and objects relative to others that remain stationary, for example an extremely fast travelling clock runs more slowly than another one at rest; a person returning from a mission in space may find him or herself biologically younger than another person stationed on earth; etc.

The microcosm is the world of reality Class III and IV. The first signs of the uncertain nature of matter are found on the Class III Level of reality, the world of atoms and molecules. The atom is the smallest unit of a chemical element and the molecule is the smallest possible portion of a particular substance, a combination of 2 or more atoms. Solid rock of reality, Class I reveals itself in Class III as frenetic, dancing bits of matter. All atoms and molecules are in constant motion. This insight convinced some scientists and ordinary people that the underlying reality of things may not be so "real" after all!

On the next step, down from the world of molecules and atoms we focus on subatomic particles of Class IV Level of Reality. As mentioned before, to get an idea of the scales involved and to justify my creation of this additional class, let us "glance" at an atom as high as a fourteen storey building. What we see is almost entirely empty space and the electrons orbiting the salt grain sized nucleus of the atom are not larger than particles of dust or, according to Ernest Rutherford who postulated the theory of the structure of the atom more than a hundred years ago, "like tiny flies in a cathedral"!

Considering the weird nature of particles, we ought to recognise Class IV as the very last outpost of reality. The realm of the quantum in general is perplexingly ethereal, a hazy field of transition between the physical, mental and the U-Minded world. It is a divide without borders and stretches from somewhere to apparent nowhere, from the uncertainty of the quantum to the world of ideas and potentialities, from ordinary space-time to the wholeness of the U-Minded world.

Quantum physics and its repercussions play such an important role in my theory of existence that it is appropriate to gain a broader perspective of its evolution, incorporating various key elements of its development.

A PINNACLE OF SCIENCE

A BRIEF HISTORY OF QUANTUM MECHANICS

It all started with Max Planck's theory of quanta in 1900 and Niels Bohr's theory of the hydrogen atom in 1913. Max Planck, a professor of physics at Berlin University discovered in October 1900 the unifying law of black body radiation. He also discovered that the black body could only absorb radiation in discrete packets and not in a steady manner as he expected. He called these packets quanta, Latin for "how much". Shortly after, he presented the Formula E = hf (E equals the energy in one of these quanta, f the frequency of radiation and h Planck's constant).

In 1905, Albert Einstein also came to the conclusion that radiation, until then regarded to be wavelike, could sometimes be regarded as minute packets of energy.

In 1913 Niels Bohr, a Danish physicist put forward an idea that an electron (a matter particle) can only have an energy that is an exact multiple of a fundamental packet, a quantum of energy, in its orbit around the nucleus of an atom. In its stable orbit an electron does not give off energy but they can be driven into higher stable orbits (or even out of the atom) by putting energy, for example heat, into the atom. On cooling, the surplus energy emerges as photons of radiant energy (light) of a certain wavelength and colour which in turn and according to Planck's formula relates exactly to the energy difference of the electron now quantum-jumping down into lower orbits.

These early pioneers of quantum mechanics really shook the pillars of the scientific establishment with their outlandish ideas because it was commonly accepted in those days that light is made up of waves. It was Christian Huygens, a Dutch physicist who is credited with the first formulation of the wave theory of light propagation in 1678. Thomas Young, an English physician and physicist proved in his light-beam interference experiment almost 150 years later beyond any reasonable doubt the wavelike nature of light.

Could radiation be both, wave and particle, at the same time? The evidence was supplied in 1923 by the American physicist Arthur Compton. He found that when X-rays were directed onto thin metal foils, some of the radiation went straight through and some was scattered (reflected). He discovered that the wave lengths of the reflected X-ray energy changed to a lower frequency because quanta of X-ray energy were driven into electrons making up the atoms in the foil. Compton realised that this experiment confirmed Planck's law of E = hf and at the same time demonstrated in detail the dual nature of all radiation.

The newly discovered wave-particle duality of radiation prompted a renewed effort in understanding the nature of wave behaviour. It was also a first step in trying to understand the perplexities of the quantum world in general.

In 1924, Niels Bohr and his colleagues H.A. Kramers and John Slater introduced the novel idea of probability waves. Unlike classical probability where, for example the chances of hitting the chosen number on a roulette wheel are one in thirty-six, this type of probability meant "a tendency to happen"; it was likely to happen, not just possible. The probability wave is a mathematical entity that enclosed, according to Heisenberg, something standing in the middle between the idea of an event and the actual event, a strange kind of physical "intermediacy" between possibility and realisation. Unfortunately, their mathematics didn't work out and it was later up to Max Born, using the mathematics of De Broglie and Schrödinger and his own simple formula, to be able to calculate a sequence of probabilities (of observations) from the initial conditions.

A French aristocrat and physicist, Prince Louis de Broglie came up with the idea that not only can waves of radiation have particle-like properties, but that particles of matter, the likes of protons and electrons, can also have wavelike properties whilst in motion.

In 1925 he formulated a simple equation, $\lambda = h/mv$. It determined the wavelength of matter waves from a combination of Planck's formula and Einstein's equation $E = mc^2$. The experimental evidence emerged in 1927 by accident when an American physicist, Clinton Davisson with his assistant, Lester Germer, beamed electrons onto a crystal of nickel. These electrons reflected off the crystal surface in a manner that could only be explained if electrons were waves, reminiscent of Thomas Young's light beam interference experiment.

The next step in the evolution of quantum mechanics was the famous Schrödinger wave equation in 1926. Erwin Schrödinger, an Austrian professor at the university of Stuttgart worked out a formula, incorporating De Broglie's ideas, mathematical wave description and a bit of simple mechanics. The central object in it was the "wave function". The wave function is a "quantity" associated with every particle. It enshrines mathematically the wavelike behaviour of a particle in motion but not the nature of the wave. Schrödinger visualised particles of matter, for example electrons, as "standing waves" but could not say what was waving. He nevertheless was convinced that these standing waves were "real", not mathematical abstractions or anything else. Schrödinger's equation was modified by Wolfgang Pauli, another Austrian physicist. He discovered that an electron with one particular set of properties (quantum numbers) excludes the presence of another electron with exactly the same properties within the same atom. His discovery became known as Pauli's exclusion principle.

Schrödinger was one of the two chief architects of the theory of quantum mechanic's technical structure, the other was the German Werner Heisenberg. In 1925, only 25 years old, Heisenberg adapted a method of collecting and setting experimental data into mathematical tables (matrices), introduced by the Irish mathematician W.R. Hamilton sixty years earlier. In his application these tables only incorporated physical observables, probabilities associated with initial conditions, things we know at the beginning and at the end of an experiment. His view was that what happens in between is pure speculation and of no concern. His scheme became known as matrix mechanics. He didn't attempt to describe what was going on in the realm of the quantum but simply dismissed the ambiguity associated with wave functions or electron clouds and declared that we never can know what actually goes on in the invisible subatomic world and therefore we should abandon all attempts to construct perceptual models of atomic processes!

Schrödinger's wave mechanics and Heisenberg's matrix mechanics are entirely different theories but produce the same mathematical result. Heisenberg was convinced that there are fundamental limits to our ability to know everything about the world and in 1927 he wrote one of the most remarkable scientific papers ever to be published, instantly and officially opening the door to a new era in science and philosophy. At that moment, the term "exact science" (as applied to physics) lost its meaning because in the realm of the quantum the rigid rules of the past do not apply any more. The "uncertainty principle" as it became known, states that it is impossible precisely to measure both, the motion <u>and</u> position of a subatomic particle. If you "zoom in" on its position (for example an electron orbiting the nucleus of an atom) you cannot say with equal precision what its velocity is and "vice versa". Mathematically, the fundamental limit to knowledge is dictated by Planck's constant.

Einstein, a physicist in the classic mould of Newton, was able to digest the concept of Schrödinger's standing waves and the wave function in his equation, but Heisenberg's declaration really rattled him. "It's a real witches calculus" he said, but Heisenberg's professor and mentor, the German physicist Max Born's interpretation of Schrödinger's reasonably solid looking wave function shook him to the core. "God does not play dice with the universe" was his now famous quotation concerning his views on uncertainty and the probabilistic nature of subatomic particles. In 1926, Born interpreted the wave association of a particle not as a physical effect (not a real thing) but as a wave of probability in which the wave function of an electron for example only gives the odds of that electron's turning up as a "real" particle at a certain place, <u>if</u> we make an attempt to look for it by means of an experiment. Schrödinger's wave function is nothing more than a mathematical device because his equation could not say exactly where the electron is, it can only give the probability of the electron's position.

Niels Bohr, who is the chief architect of quantum mechanic's interpretation, quickly adopted and extended this theory which, in 1927, became known as the "Copenhagen interpretation". It was the result of great debates between the leading physicists of the first half of the twentieth century. Bohr published a manifesto in which he firmly planted the idea of particle/wave duality on a solid foundation. He explained that the wavelike behaviour (as in the Davisson Experiment for example) or the particle like behaviour (as in collision and scattering experiments) are complementary aspects of a quantum object's fundamental nature. Also, no experiment can give us information about the two behaviour patterns simultaneously because, and this is of profound importance, it is the act of observation that brings the thing we observe into existence ...., it transforms the unpredictable "fuzzy, wavy thing" into measurable "real objects". It also implies that there is no physical reality independent of humans.

The "Copenhagen Interpretation" says further that what we perceive to be physical reality is actually our cognitive construction of it, it may appear to be substantive but in actual fact is not at all what it appears.

The interesting part of the "Copenhagen Interpretation" is the elucidation of the nature of the raw-state electron before an observation is done. It suggests that it cannot be said to exist at any place or in any discrete material form at all outside the probabilistic description given by the wave function and the wave function says that it exists only as an endlessly proliferating number of possibilities generated in accordance with the Schrödinger wave equation. In other words, until the moment a particle is observed, it has no definite position or motion; it is everywhere and nowhere in particular, we cannot even regard it as being a particle. According to Bohr we have to disrupt its raw state, meaning, we have to carry out an experimental observation or measurement for the so called particle to lose its wavy-fuzzy ghost like nature and "make up its mind" what it is going to do. Physics cannot answer questions about its individual nature when it is not under observation.

"Uncertainty" is the central tenet of the Copenhagen Interpretation.

Bohr was convinced that whatever we try, we will never know with complete accuracy all there is to know about the behaviour of a particle. All we can do is to use Schrödinger's equation or equivalent means to determine the odds that an electron for example is at a particular place at a particular time.

Considering that the wave or particle-like behaviour of a quantum object are complementary aspects of its nature, it is simply impossible that an electron for example, could have conventional, objective existence. However, "it" exists.

So, what exactly could have left those visible marks (in the shape of tiny dots) after an electron passed through the photographic plate inside a bubble chamber? If a particle in its raw state has no objective, independent existence of its own, could they be manifestations of interacting fields?

The foundation stones of quantum field theory and of specific importance, the theory of quantum electro-dynamics, QED for short, were laid in 1928 by the enigmatic English physicist Paul Dirac. The original quantum field theory stipulates that fields are the "true substance" of our universe. Particles are simply manifestations of interacting fields. Their interactions in specific experiments seem to be particle-like because fields interact abruptly and in minute regions of space.

The concept of quantum field was introduced because it could successfully explain existing particles in terms of field interactions and later was successful in predicting new types of particles. As Dirac only had to deal with three types of particles, he allocated a field to each one of them. This idea was later abandoned because of the "congestion" caused by the discovery of hundreds of other types of particles. Today they recognise a quantum field as an area of influence caused by particle interaction, for example electromagnetism. For Dirac though, those visible "tracks" on the photographic plate were created by interactions of quantum fields. QED is part of quantum field theory and deals specifically with the motion (dynamics) of particles (electrons, photons and positrons) in the presence of an electro-magnetic field. It is fundamentally a theory of how electrons (particles of matter) interact with photons (particles of radiation such as light). It is also a mathematical account of the basic physics behind everything, from the atomic nucleus to an entire planet; for example wherever we are, the environment (furniture, a mountain etc.) is filled with electrons (in matter), interacting with light.

Dirac was the first person to bring together special relativity, quantum theory and electromagnetic phenomena in a complex mathematical equation. On imposing the requirements of relativity, Dirac's theory revealed something extraordinary. In his equation, one of two solutions described the behaviour of an electron, but the other solution described the behaviour of a positively charged particle, first thought to be the proton. Shortly after its discovery it became evident that it was a new particle with exactly the same mass as an electron but opposite electric charge. In 1931, Dirac boldly announced that according to his equations, every particle in the universe has a counterpart, **an Antiparticle.**

(A few particles are their own antiparticles, for example the photon and the graviton).

The evidence of this new particle's existence came as early as 1932. Unaware of Dirac's announcement, an American physicist, Carl David Anderson, while doing research on cosmic rays, discovered a particle identical to the one described by Dirac and called it the positron, reflecting the fact that it has a positive charge.

Despite the early successes of Dirac's original conception of QED, by the late 1940's it began to run into trouble. Practical experiments showed a discrepancy of 118 parts in 100 000 in the magnetic strength of an electron in his equation. This was the first out-break of the mathematical infinity disease that was going to plague theoreticians for decades. Nevertheless, the problem for specific theories (incl. QED) was soon solved when first the Japanese Sin-Itiro Tomonaga in 1943 and then independently the two Americans Julian Schwinger and Richard Feynman in 1949 found a way of getting around the dreaded infinity disease. Feynman's diagram didn't seem to be related to Tomonaga and Schwinger's mathematics but the end result was essentially the same. The "cure" for the disease was called re-normalisation. Feynman's diagrams proved themselves to be more popular in the long run and helped pave the way for QED to become one of the most successful theories. What Feynman actually discovered was that space-time maps depicting things in space and their location in time correspond to mathematical expressions which give the probabilities of their interactions. Feynman's diagrams are not limited to QED, they accommodate all particle activities and interactions.

A bit earlier, in 1936, a Hungarian-American mathematician, John von Neumann and his colleague Garrett Birkhoff published a paper "The Logic of Quantum Mechanics". In it they disproved the universality of classical logic and asserted the fact that experience and logic do not always follow the same rules. To demonstrate their theory they used polarized light and some mathematics to disprove one of the foundations of classical logic, the law of distributivity (A, and B or C equals A and B or A and C). Although von Neumann's approach to the creation of a separate science of reasoning confined to the realm of the quantum caused a great deal of confusion among his contemporaries, he nevertheless left his mark, proving that our basic thought processes are extremely restrictive when applied to different levels of reality.

As mentioned previously, the central tenet of the Copenhagen interpretation of quantum mechanics is the unavoidability of uncertainty. Albert Einstein never accepted this statement. For him everything is certain if the hidden variables are known, scientists just don't try hard enough to find them! Like a man possessed he attacked Bohr's views. These imaginative assaults were delivered by way of thought experiments. The most notable one was when he, in 1935, together with his colleagues Boris Podolsky and Nathan Rosen published their EPR thought experiment titled "Can quantum mechanical description of physical reality be considered complete? ". Their specific target was Bohr's claim that particles do not have definite properties until someone makes an observation of them. Einstein believed that the quantum theory is not a "complete" theory because it does not describe certain aspects of reality.

Their experiment-strategy was: If we cannot directly determine the position and the momentum of one particle, all we need is a second particle whose motion, by the law of action and reaction (which also applies to quantum particles), can be linked to the first particle in advance. There is a simple way to achieve this. Just visualise an exploding two-particle molecule in which the two particles fly off in opposite directions. The momentum of particle "one" can be measured and this enables us, by the law of action and reaction, to deduce the momentum of particle "two". If we simultaneously measure the position of particle "two", then we know both, the position and the momentum of particle "two".

Two assumptions are playing a crucial role in this experiment. The first is that a particle has a separate and independent position and momentum even when no observation is made and the second; they will have to be separated by a great distance to minimise interaction or communication between the two. Any signalling or other influence must be restricted to the speed of light. Bohr's general view of this experiment was that using an accomplice particle was tantamount to cheating. He maintained that if you make a measurement on one particle, the other particle, by the principle of uncertainty, remains ghostlike and its position uncertain until a measurement is made. Most importantly, there is no guarantee that the act of measuring had no influence on its ghostly partner, even at a great distance; in fact, Bohr supports the view that the fuzziness of unobserved particles proves that they are not separate, independent entities at all but are part of a holistic system.

Arguments provoked counter arguments and after a while, the intellectual battle between these giants became deadlocked. Einstein's views gradually lost their appeal and for many physicists he began to look like a spent force in the world of physical science. The Copenhagen interpretation with all its peculiar notions and paradoxes came out the winner. But there was no proof and no way yet to prove it until 1964 when John S. Bell, a British physicist at the Centre for European Nuclear Research (CERN) in Geneva published a mathematical statement which became known as "Bell's Theorem".

This breakthrough opened the way for a future experimental "set-up" to provide conclusive evidence not only for or against what the Copenhagen interpretation of quantum mechanics stands for, for example Bohr's view on the unavoidability of uncertainty, but also for or against his conviction that at a fundamental level all the separate parts of our universe are connected in an intimate and immediate way.

Bell worked out a mathematical statement for the degree of particle co-operation expected according to Einstein's theory and then according to Bohr's quantum mechanics.

He took the two basic assumptions in the EPR thought experiment (objective reality and no signalling or any other influence travelling faster than light) and used these conditions to calculate a limit (a kind of bench mark) to the degree of co-operation expected between two separated particles, similar to the pair of hypothetical particles used in the EPR thought experiment.

After giving his attention to the "Copenhagen Interpretation" and taking Bohr's view of quantum uncertainty and his strong feelings in favour of instantaneous particle interaction into account, he was not surprised that the degree of cooperation between the two particles exceeded Einstein's set limits. - Why? Quite simply; Einstein's "Hidden Variables" could only operate at maximum the speed of light!

Bell's mathematical construct, indecipherable to a layman but recognised as one of the great theories of physics, was ready and waiting to be tested.

In 1972, the American physicists, John Clauser and Stuart Freedman at the Lawrence Berkely Laboratory performed a test using paired photons (particles of light). The result confirmed that Bohr's view of quantum mechanics was correct but the experiment was flawed as it did not indicate if the high degree of cooperation was due to conventional or faster than the speed of light communication (measurements were not spacelike separated).

Finally, in 1982, eighteen years after John Bell published his theorem, the French physicist Alain Aspect and his team at the University of Paris carried out the most sophisticated experiment yet performed. He used the same method as Clauser and Freedman but incorporated some major improvements.

His set-up was designed for two photons to emerge from a central source and travel for six metres in opposite directions through an optical gate that diverted the photons in one of two directions. The gates could be randomly switched at great speed whilst the photons were in full flight, their destination unknown at any time before the switch.

The experimental set-up made it impossible for one photon to know what happened to the other via speed of light communication. Their final destination after passing through polarisers and photo multipliers was the coincidence detector. The results were startling. The degree of cooperation and/or communication was five times higher than the set limit expected according to Einstein's view of reality but was more or less the amount predicted using Bohr's view of quantum mechanics. The Aspect experiment therefore successfully disproved Einstein's "Reality Views" of quantum theory and explicitly confirmed that common sense ideas of the quantum world and indirectly our world in general, are totally inadequate. However, it still left scientists with more questions than answers because science in general is steeped in tradition and tries to solve problems within the boundaries of ordinary space and time. Some of the more pertinent questions are:

Can particles truly communicate faster than the speed of light or what alternative could explain the above phenomenon?

Is the uncertainty principle still valid in view of instantaneous communication?

What is the true behaviour of unobserved particles and couldn't "hidden variables" still play a role in explaining particle behaviour?

What Bell's theorem and Aspect's experiment has revealed is that subatomic particles, however spacelike separated, are firmly **linked,** proving beyond all reasonable doubt the underlying unity of the universe.

David Bohm, a professor of physics at Birkbeck College, University of London, displayed remarkable courage and creative spirit in not blindly following the crowd of physicists gathering behind Bohr and his "Copenhagen Interpretation". He reiterated Bell's and Bohr's strong belief that everything is part of an unbroken wholeness but was not at all happy with Heisenberg's Uncertainty principle adopted by Niels Bohr, Max Born and followers. He worked on a new theory that could explain quantum uncertainty, eliminate its principle and re-create a kind of "reality" in the weird world of subatomic particles.

In the early 1950's he announced to the scientific community that every particle is influenced by something described as Hidden Variable, something that dictates how particles behave and he termed it "The Quantum Potential". Its mathematical form was clearly defined and it fitted well into the existing quantum theory.

In essence, the Quantum Potential links all particles together in an immense, interconnected web of non-causal, non-local relationships enabling unlimited and instantaneous communication. According to Bohm there ought to be no conflict with Einstein's special theory of relativity as it is not applicable (valid) at the deeper level at which the Quantum Potential exerts its influence. He maintains that its influence alone is responsible for quantum uncertainty, it affects the "well defined classical behaviour" of a particle in such a way that if we zoom in on its position for example, we cannot determine with equal precision its momentum and vice-versa. The observed fuzziness is an effect and the cause is the influence of the Quantum Potential. He mentions that quantum uncertainty is not intrinsic but the result of fluctuations in the Quantum Potential. According to Bohm, if someone makes a measurement extremely fast or over an extremely small distance, it may be possible to pin down the momentum and position of a particle more accurately. On a more philosophical note Bohm reveals that the unbroken wholeness of our universe quite simply is "that which is"! Everything, including space, time and matter are forms of "that which is". There is an order enfolded into the very process of our universe but this may not be readily apparent. This is the "Implicate Order". Particles are also forms of the "Implicate Order". They may be discontiguous (not touching) in space (the "Explicate Order") but contiguous (touching) in the "Implicate Order".

Bohm emphasises that there is a similarity between thought and matter. All matter, including ourselves, is determined by information. Information is what determines space and time.

Unfortunately, Bohm's quantum ideas did not please Einstein, primarily because it incorporated faster than light cooperation and his comments on the Quantum Potential was: "It is the product of not looking deep enough into the nature of reality".

His ideas of the "Quantum Potential" were simply dismissed by Bohr and most of his followers including the well-known physicist Robert Oppenheimer.

Oppenheimer, on being confronted by students at a seminar was quoted as saying "we can't really find anything wrong with it, so we will just have to ignore it!"

A notable exception to Bohr's ignorant physicist followers was the mathematician, physicist and thinker, John Bell, whose theorem was compatible with Bohm's theory.

In 1957, the American physicist Hugh Everett claimed that wave functions never collapse (the collapse of the wave function is based on the Copenhagen interpretation of quantum mechanics), but decompose by splitting apart into different worlds (that co-exist with ours) every time a quantum interaction (observed or not!) takes place. The splitting takes account of all the possible outcomes (all the possibilities that can happen) as represented by the wave function.

Everett also claims that when a wave function splits, all the possibilities become realities in their own respective "real worlds". He implies that all we are aware of is only what actually happens in our own world and this only under certain circumstances (at the conclusion of an observation!).

If we are to believe this theory, the mind boggles at the number of "real" worlds out there because quantum interactions in our physical world, undiscerned by our eyes, are happening an incredible number of times every second. Amazingly, some leading quantum scientists were prepared to accept this theory for lack of a more "realistic" alternative to the problem of measurement.

The "faster than the speed of light communication/co-operation" between space-like separated particles as predicted by Bohr's quantum theory and incorporated in Bohm's Quantum Potential in the early 1950's served as an incentive for further theories that postulated non-causal connections between space-like separated events in the world of the quantum.

In 1975, the American physicist Jack Sarfatti proposed a theory under the strange name of "Superluminal transfer of negentropy without signals" (Negentropy being the opposite of entropy, meaning disorder; signal means transfer of energy through space-time. Increasing entropy is manifest in the second law of Thermodynamics). The superluminal (faster than light) information transfer without signals ought to solve the problem posed by the theory of relativity that stipulates that any communication between spacelike separated particles requires a "signal" that can only travel at maximum the speed of light.

Sarfatti also states that a "quantum jump" (at the collapse of a wave function) is a faster than light change of particle state with no transfer of energy although, there will be a change in the coherent structure of the actualised particle.

Another American physicist, Henry P. Stapp, published a paper in 1977, expressing his theory of superluminal connections entitled: "Are Superluminal Connections Necessary?" and I quote: "Everything about nature is in accordance with the idea that the fundamental processes of nature lie outside space-time but generate events that can be located in space-time". The theory of his paper supports this view by showing that superluminal transfer of information is necessary, barring certain alternatives …. that seem less reasonable, and further: "Indeed, the philosophical position of Bohr seems to lead to the rejection of the other possibilities and hence, by inference, to the conclusion that superluminal transfer of information is necessary".

THE WAVE FUNCTION*

is the central mathematical element in quantum mechanics. It is also the most important source of the abstract qualities of one of the most poignant examples of abstract existent entities, the raw state particle (Group 2, Type "A" & "B".

As mentioned before Erwin Schrödinger invented this mathematical "entity" as part of his wave-equation. The wave function is a quantity that in his opinion enshrines the observational fact of the wavelike behaviour (a development of standing waves, constantly changing and proliferating) associated with every particle in motion. He didn't know what was waving but imagined that these

---

*   Technically known as the "State Vector Reduction".

waves were real (he initially suggested that it may be the electron's smeared-out charge as it moves through space).

Max Born dismissed these views and boldly stated that the wave association of a particle is not physical but a mathematical abstraction, a wave of probability. Only an act of observation brings the "thing" into existence!

Most physicists are now convinced that the wave function is a purely mathematical construction that doesn't represent anything real but represents all the possibilities that can happen to an "observed system" (physicist's Jargon for the particle/wave) before it interacts with an "observing system" (e.g. a measuring device, a photographic plate or a technician etc.). It allows the scientist to determine the <u>probable</u> outcome of the interaction. Fact is that the "observed system" cannot be observed until it interacts with the "observing system" and even then the scientist or technician can only observe it's physical <u>effects</u> on a measuring device.

We must always keep in mind that terms, the likes of "observed system", "observing system" and also waves, particles, fuzz, particle cloud, field, photon, electron etc. are just meaningful and useful words to enable us to communicate with one another.

The wave function deals with possibilities. To reflect adequately the range of possibilities (in some instances a vast range) open to the particle, for example that the particle in motion will be detected in Area "A" or "B" or "C" on a photographic plate, the wave function must take the form of three individual wave function, a composite of three possibilities constantly changing and developing according to Schrödinger's wave equation. Among physicists it is called a "superposition of wave function". It is the mathematical soul of quantum mechanics. All wave functions are coherent super-positions. To form an image of a wave function think of it as a dynamic double or triple (or more) exposure on a "not so still" photograph!

The form of the wave function is calculated by way of the Schrödinger wave equation for any moment between the time a particle leaves the set-up region and the time that it interacts with the measuring device. The wave equation also contains all the experimental specifications. By squaring the amplitude of the (now calculated) wave function, the physicist creates a second mathematical "entity", <u>the probability function</u>. This function tells him the probabilities (in classical language "the odds" that this or that will happen) at a given time of each of the possibilities represented by the wave function. Quantum mechanics does not predict what will happen, only the probabilities of various possible results. If he knows the initial conditions and specifications of the experiment and uses the natural causal laws of development, he will be able to calculate exactly the probability for a certain result to occur, for example that there is a 45 percent probability that the particle will be detected in area "A", 35 percent in Area "B" and 20 percent in Area "C".

But what determines where the particle will be detected?

The quantum theory (according to the Copenhagen interpretation) says: "pure chance". Einstein says: "God does not play dice" and my answer is: "Where the particle will be detected depends on results of "super luminal" Communication – Computation activity in the wholeness of the U-minded world as suggested in more physical terms by Bell's theorem and other quantum science related theories. It is not a matter of pure chance. In the greater scheme,

> the C.-C. signal network is ultimately influenced and to a certain point controlled by the natural tendency of the universal mind (via "Potentia") to fulfil its primary purpose:

"Optimal Existence" and continuity thereof ......

It is clear that the wave function is a human invented mathematical creation, the result of applied mathematics at its brilliant best (applied mathematics is the science of magnitude and numbers in which known relations are subjected to certain processes that enable other relations to be deduced, applied to concrete data of observed facts of nature!). When Schrödinger "worked out" the wave function, he took existing scientific facts and ideas (De Broglie's ideas, mathematical wave description and some simple mechanics) and combined them according to his own experiences and ideas and "voila", the central mathematical element in quantum theory was born.

In the creation of this mathematical abstraction, the human mind was the key because only the mind can perceive the subtle interconnections of nature. The human brain receives and absorbs external facts and ideas for the mind to assess, visualise, compare, modify and conclude. However, long before it was also the human mind that recognised the laws, rules and the order of the external world as well as qualities and characteristics of things within and again it was the human mind that invented meaningful words, numbers and symbols to match the above.

Statements that the wave function is "matter-like" or reflects reality are based on wrong assumptions or false information. Apart from its mathematical usefulness, the wave function <u>reflects the uncertain nature of the quantum</u> and suggests a raw state particle's "mode of existence". According to the Copenhagen interpretation: It exists only in the way the wave function suggests and the wave function says that it only exists as an "endlessly proliferating number of possibilities". Hence, all raw state particles have the quality of being **multifaceted Potentialities,** harnessed, constrained and limited by the rules and laws of physics (and scientific experiments!) and their mode of being is: "Abstract Existent".

Mathematically, the wave function represents all the possibilities that can happen to the particle before it interacts with an observing system.

The act of observation/measuring or detection triggers the **Collapse of the Wave Function!**

It sounds overdramatized but the statement is justified in view of the fact that the collapse is an abrupt particle transition from an abstract existent entity to a "real" Class IV entity. The word "collapse" does not depict anything real. It is a mental image, sometimes referred to as a quantum leap. It signifies the **Transition of a raw state particle from a multifaceted potentiality to a single actuality.**

It is the abrupt collapse of all the developing aspects of the wave function with the exception of the one that actualises. The quantum leap also signifies the transition from a potentiality with a theoretically infinite number of dimensions into reality (Class IV) which has only three plus time.

Let us consider a wave function that contains three possibilities (a superposition of three individual wave functions), for example for possible particle detection in Areas A, B or C of a photographic plate. This wave function is a mathematical entity with three different developments simultaneously in nine different dimensions plus time. At the precise moment of detection we reduce the multidimensional potentiality to a three dimensional reality plus time, compatible with our experience. Bohr stated that whenever we carry out a measurement on a particle, it can no longer enjoy the run of all the possible states that the wave function implies. It must stop being a ghost. All wave functions that make up the superposition must collapse except for one that is raised to a special status that allows us, within limits, to say what the particle is doing now that it is under scientific observation. The most intriguing question among quantum theorists is:

When exactly does a wave function collapse?

Bohr stated that a wave function collapses whenever we carry out a measurement or valid quantum observation on a particle, but what exactly constitutes a valid quantum observation or measurement?

Opinions differ widely. Some theorists say that a wave function collapses when a particle strikes the photographic plate, in other words as soon as a measuring apparatus, unattended by a human, automatically registers an impact. Others say that it is human consciousness that brings about the collapse of the wave function. According to the Hungarian-American mathematician John von Neumann, the main requirement is the exclusion of the measuring apparatus from the wave function of the system being observed.

In principle, the whole problem arises because of the interconnectedness of nature. In the words of a well-known quantum physicist: "Being part of the macrocosm, the microcosm (the world of the quantum) is a network of relations, an all-encompassing and inseparable web of superluminal connections of information and dynamic exchanges of energy".

Matter is made up of atoms and atoms are made up of particles that can all be described by wave functions themselves. Looking at it from this perspective, the measuring apparatus or whatever does the observation or measurement, could then also be described by wave functions. However, a wave function cannot be made to collapse by another overlapping and interfering wave function. In scientific circles the dispute is appropriately known as the "Measurement Problem".

Hugh Everett proposed a theory that obliterated the problem of measurement in its entirety. This rather audacious conjecture is known as the "Many Worlds Theory".

My opinion is that John von Neumann's views are correct and there is no further need to delve any deeper into the subject-matter. At present we still have no way of getting to know the underlying laws governing the so-called "Network of Relations" and the "Web of superluminal connections of information".

SUBATOMIC PARTICLE CLASSIFICATION

In keeping with the theme of this book I categorised all known particles according to their levels of existence. They are divided into two main groups, the so called "real" particles and the "abstract existent":

GROUP 1: SUBATOMIC PARTICLES BELONGING TO EXISTENCE LEVEL "A", REALITY CLASS IV.

Type "A":

Stable particle and anti-particle entities, detected, observed and measured in scientific experiments by means of an "observing system". Their actual existence is verified by means of, for example, a physical trace on a photographic plate. The analysis ought to reveal a particle's identity from its trace characteristics.

Although this particular category may appear controversial, I don't think there is a more fitting moment to proclaim the emergence of reality than at the very instant of a particle's wave function collapse. The traces on a photographic plate for example are first signs of its actual, factual and true existence. It may still not reveal form or structure but it has given away identity and location and, most importantly, it is recognised as one of the fundamental building blocks of nature. Because of its borderline status, I confine this group of particles to the bottom of existence level "A", reality Class IV.

Quarks are not yet included in Group 1 as they have never been seen individually, as separate parts of protons and neutrons.

Type "B":

As above but medium-stable particle and antiparticles entities, e.g. "free" neutrons (15 min.).

Type "C":

As above but unstable particle and antiparticle entities.

GROUP 2: SUBATOMIC PARTICLES BELONGING TO EXISTENCE LEVEL "C", ABSTRACT EXISTENCE CLASS II.

Type "A":

Stable particle and anti particle entities in any raw, natural state before any observation or measurement has been done (before their wave function collapse). Any such particle is classified as abstract existent because its mode of being and behaviour is steeped in uncertainty. It exists in abstract mode on existence level "C", Class II for the duration of its existence or until the moment of observation/measurement. According to the Copenhagen interpretation of quantum mechanics, the raw state particle does not exist at any particular place or in any discrete material form at all. It exists only in the way the wave function describes it and it suggests that it only exists as an endlessly proliferating number of possibilities (as a multifaceted potentiality!).

Type "B":

As above but medium-stable.

Type "C":

As above but unstable.

Type "D":

Virtual particles of force fields. Force carrier particles come in two types, stable for electromagnetism and gravity (Type "A") and virtual for all subatomic forces, for example strong and weak nuclear as well as electromagnetic forces. Virtual force carrier particles are emitted and absorbed by subatomic particles, constantly flitting to and from particle to particle.

NOTE: Because of their common wave-particle duality (which introduces a degree of unification), I did not differentiate between matter particles and particles of force fields, with the exception of Type "D" (Group 2) which needed special mention because of its unique situation.

This note applies for Group 1 and 2 particles.

GROUP 3: VACUUM PARTICLES BELONGING TO EXISTENCE LEVEL "C", ABSTRACT EXISTENCE CLASS II.

Quantum theory tells us that the vacuum of empty space, devoid of ordinary matter and radiation, is not at all what it appears to be. Apart from dark matter and radiation, is not at all what it appears to be. Apart from dark matter and dark energy (of which not much information exists), the vacuum of "empty" space ought to be a seething ferment of so-called virtual particle and antiparticle pairs of all types, constantly creating and annihilating each other. However, as measured by astronomers, this evanescent activity is currently not as strong as expected.

Virtual vacuum particles are mathematically entrenched mental products, part of the energy scheme of our physical world but occupy a twilight zone between "normal" (not real!) raw type particles and "Potentia" in the wholeness of the U-minded world.

Virtual vacuum particles behave similarly to virtual particles of force fields but have only "Potentia" at their "ends" whereas virtual particles of force-fields have subatomic particles (e.g. electrons and quarks) at their ends to come from and go to.

This classification serves as a rough guide. It would be interesting to see a particle or string/brane classification compiled in similar Order of Being by an expert physicist.

2

MACRO MOVEMENTS

THE POSITIVE AND NEGATIVE PHASES
OF COSMIC EXPANSION & CONTRACTION

Currently, energy on a cosmic scale is stored in the gravitational attraction between galaxies and clusters of galaxies, in their motion (kinetic energy), in the gravitational attraction of dark matter (forming extended halos around galaxies) and the previously mentioned vacuum energy. However, the most significant energy at present, distributed evenly throughout the physical world, is the newly "introduced" dark energy.

Galactic clusters and most galaxies are moving away from one another, meaning, the physical world as a whole is expanding. The driving outward force (repulsive force) is believed to be exerted by the dark energy (in conjunction with the kinetic energy of outward moving galaxies and clusters of galaxies).

Opposing this movement and thereby preventing a catastrophic runaway expansion are the binding gravitational forces exerted by galaxies in conjunction with the binding gravitational pull of dark matter.

The **positive*** outward pushing forces and the **negative** inward pulling gravitational forces are **the two opposing factors** that today, to our knowledge, are accountable for the overall dynamics of our physical world.

---

*   In my view, the cosmic expansion is directly responsible for the (positive) natural development within.

According to Albert Einstein, our physical world, in essence, is space-time activity.

Space-time is elastic, it can change and move. It can stretch and expand but also shrink and therefore contract. The physical world is now in a (positive) phase of accelerating expansion.

Bending or warping is caused by the localised gravity of stars, planets etc. Einstein explains that a piece of matter is a "curvature of the space-time continuum".

Distortion occurs in the vicinity of a black hole. Extreme localised gravity of massive dying stars are causing grotesquely distorted local space prisons. On the quantum scale, mathematical modelling suggests that space-time will become foamy, frothlike in structure with violent, spontaneous growth and decay of curvature. On this ultra-microscopic scale, space-time explores all the pathways of motion available to it.

As previously mentioned, the physical world is now in a phase of accelerating cosmic expansion. The big question is: Will optimal conditions for natural development continue for the foreseeable future or will the physical world undergo a runaway expansion? If the universe was under human control, I would have my doubts. Fortunately, the universe controls itself by means of its own universal mind, and quite successfully so far. Right from the "beginning" it seems to have been set on a path of optimal conditions for its survival and development. The conventional big bang theory suggests that ideally balanced conditions prevented the "early" physical world from either collapsing or from a runaway expansion and subsequent early annihilation. If the force of the big bang would have been less vigorous, the negative force of gravity would have taken hold of the expanding space-time, reversed its motion and engulfed the early world in a premature catastrophic implosion. Instead we experience now, billions of years later, accelerating but still optimum cosmic expansion, **favouring a certain degree of permanence.**

The human race and other forms of life enjoy now the benefits of a finely tuned cosmic expansion. It provided space, matter and radiation with adequate time to organise itself and bring forth unimaginable development.

Finely tuned cosmic expansion is inextricably linked to the preponderance of physical world order and development over degeneration, chaos, collapse and disintegration.

The physical world will go on expanding for many millions of years before slowing down dramatically, and then, after the period of equilibrium (the physical world's era of fulfilment!), it will set course for its return, inward journey.

This theory opposes the views expressed by adherents of the standard big bang model. Dark energy was introduced to explain the physical world's current accelerating expansion. For the followers of the standard big bang model, dark energy and the kinetic energy of expansion will dominate the future of our world, a future that inevitably would end in that from which it originally created itself - "nothing"!

Even before the introduction of dark energy, leading scientists maintained the view that the physical world would keep on expanding, indefinitely, mainly because their calculations showed that the density of matter did not exceed a critical level of approximately seven protons per cubic-meter. The actual density of all matter in the physical world was calculated by estimating the number of galaxies in the visible cosmos multiplied by the average number of stars in each galaxy, multiplied by the average mass of a star and divided by the volume of the visible cosmos. The resultant figure of 0.1 protons per cubic-meter was thus far below the critical value of seven protons per cubic-meter. When dark matter is taken into account, the figure rises to one proton per cubic meter. Particle physicists also contributed and included weakly interacting massive particles (WIMP's). These are theoretical products of the idea of supersymmetry. Calculations revealed that the total mass of even the lightest of these supersymmetric partners of ordinary matter could be high enough to help reverse the expansion of the physical world. This warranted a massive search for these particles but so far all attempts to verify their existence proved fruitless.

The majority of physicists and astronomers considered the evidence supporting a long slow death by long-lasting expansion as sufficient to accept this scenario as the most likely outcome. However, with the introduction of dark energy to explain accelerating cosmic expansion, this may have changed. For them the end (an eternal, dark, vacuous wasteland) may come a few million years sooner than anticipated!

It is widely accepted that our physical world eventually, after a great length of time, will be involved in some kind of demise or, alternatively, end in "death". The question of how it will end and whether the demise or "death" will be permanent or just a (pre-) condition for renewal is still wide open to widespread scientific and philosophical speculation.

My view is that conditions for optimal natural development will continue for millions of years. Thereafter, cosmic expansion will slow down. I will give some of my philosophical reasons for the eventual expansion slowdown and the following cosmic contraction later in this book, however, on a more scientific level, one of the reasons for the future expansion slow-down may be fundamental changes (decay) in the make-up of dark energy. The changes may transform the gravitationally self-repulsive energy into a form of extreme high pressure energy causing it and all widespread matter, to contract.

With the discovery of dark matter and the introduction of dark energy, most astronomers and astrophysicists are ready to admit that the "real" world out there is starting to look much more complex than previously imagined.

Cosmic expansion and a simultaneous preponderance of development over decay within the expansion will continue until the **inherent potential of our physical world is realised!**

The period between slowing cosmic expansion and the beginning of contraction will be the physical world's **"Era of Fulfilment"**

It will not only be the time of maximum cosmic expansion (which in itself is fulfilment in the true sense of the word) but if development still outweighs degeneration and decay during the later stages of the positive phase (cosmic expansion), then subordinated and intelligent life will in all likelihood adapt to changing circumstances. Some of it may progress beyond the scope of our imagination. There may be intelligent life scattered around the physical world capable of relationships across cosmic space via instant transfer of feelings and thought. However, long before, super humans and/or other intelligent beings may have had the ability to manipulate ordinary space-time. Artificially created space-time tunnels may have allowed these beings to translocate themselves across vast distances of space.

The "era of fulfilment" will be the pinnacle of physical world development. Cosmic expansion, evolution, growth and "progress" will have reached their theoretical and practical limits. It will be the end of **the positive phase of our cycle of physical existence and the beginning of the negative phase.**

The wide-spread physical world will succumb to ever increasing contraction caused, either by the decay of unstable dark energy, or by the gravity of the theoretically known, but not yet discovered WIMP's (weakly interacting massive particles), or even by the growing influence of a parallel physical world with opposite properties to our positive energy/matter world! Other, hereto unknown factors may also contribute or even cause the reversal of the cosmic expansion.

With the cessation of cosmic expansion, general conditions will inevitably deteriorate.

The negative phase of cosmic contraction will be inextricably linked to the preponderance of physical world degeneration, chaos and decay over order and development.

The most likely outcome of such condition is that the overpowering force of cosmic contraction will, after a considerable length of time, effectuate a **Big Crunch.**

Whatever form the crunch takes, it will be a kind of fusion of all forms of energy and forces into the quintessence of physical existence. Simultaneously, the big crunch will induce yet another **Big Bang.**

However, if the conventional big bang model (the theory of the beginning or creation of our physical world, in which Allan Guth's inflation theory is the central element) is scientifically proven to be correct, the big crunch, in my view, would effectively end in a **Transubstantiation** (Substantia would change into U-minded substance - Energy into Potentia*) for the minutest length of time and, inevitably, cause the much publicised physical "nothingness" (out of which the "one and only universe" was supposed to have been created!).

---

*   Science does not yet have a valid answer (based on irrefutable evidence) to explain the paradoxes of appearance (e.g. standard inflation theory) or disappearances (e.g. black holes) of matter ex or in "nihilo"!

Simultaneously, an "overload reaction" (imbalance) in the U-minded world would immediately trigger a quantum fluctuation in the quantum vacuum of empty space followed by the development of an unstable false vacuum etc.

In both instances (in the cyclic world model and the metaphysically modified cyclic inflation theory) the big crunch will be <u>the end of our present cycle of physical existence.</u> The simultaneous big bang will cause a re-formation and re-appearance of energy, forces and matter, possibly slightly altered but the universal mind (via "Potentia") will still be in control of the overall dynamics of a **new physical world.**

The Principle of existence and its inherent irreversible effects are anchored on the highest level ('Y') of existence, beyond ordinary space-time and even beyond the realm of the U-Minded world. As far as our physical world is concerned, there can be only one way:

Everlasting Movements.

The physical world cannot end in a final long drawn-out death by cosmic expansion. Apart from the obvious message contained in the principle of existence and other reasons, the following considerations helped cement my conviction that the physical world is not doomed to everlasting dissolution:

a) The unity of our physical world,
b) Balance,
c) Limited human knowledge.

A.   THE UNITY OF OUR PHYSICAL WORLD

Beneath the impressionable number and variety of galaxies, stars and planets and the diversity, abundance and richness of nature, exists **an all-Pervasive Unity.**

This is certainly not the impression we get in everyday life. It is quite obvious that the world outside ourselves consists of a multitude of separate entities and forms. However, science tells us otherwise. The scientific picture of our physical world is one of uniformity, coherence, large-scale simplicity and unity and the branch of physical science responsible for the enlightenment is quantum mechanics.

Max Planck initiated quantum mechanics in 1900 with his theory of quanta and later Niels Bohr became the theory's chief interpreter. These pioneers of quantum mechanics noticed a strange relationship during some of their experiments, inter alia, an incredible "Connection" or "Connectedness" among quantum phenomena.

In 1964, J.S. Bell, a physicist at Cern in Switzerland, published mathematical proof of this fact in a theory which became known as "Bell's Theorem". In its present form it is one of the most important works of physical science. A consequence of Bell's theory is that **all separate entities in our physical world are related or connected to each other at a deep and fundamental level, in an intimate and direct way.**

Neils Bohr, the Danish physicist and leading authority on the conceptual foundations of quantum mechanics reveals (in connection with an important experiment), that just because two particles have moved a long way apart, we cannot consider them as separate and independent physical entities, they remain part of a unified whole. This was in direct conflict with Albert Einstein's view which was one of objective reality, meaning each particle exists by moving along, not unpredictable, but well defined paths under the action of forces and as an independent part of a whole. Although Einstein did some pioneering work on the quantum theory, he was totally against quantum uncertainty. French physicist Alain Aspect and his team undertook in 1982 an historic experiment which proved without any doubt that Einstein's views were wrong. Quantum uncertainty was intrinsic and irreducible. The experiment not only tested the validity of quantum uncertainty, **it also showed an incredible correlation between two apparently separate particles, so much that one could assume that they are co-operating by means of telepathy or faster than light signalling.**

Their "decisions" seem to relate to "decisions" made elsewhere, possibly as far away as another planet or galaxy - at an instant!

The assumption of faster than light signalling arises because the whole of our physical world is, in essence, ordinary space-time activity in which nothing travels faster than light. Humans are part of it and in close company with fauna and flora. They live in this uniquely crafted cocoon in a world of "naive" reality, unable to see the unbound vastness of the "beyond". If they could, they would recognise that it is not mere signals that keep particles in touch but a special "environment" in which the rules and laws of physics do not longer apply, a realm in which all particles are linked. We are not familiar with this mysterious "beyond" but results of quantum scientific experiments force us to recognise subatomic particles not only as individual building blocks of matter, radiation and forces but as **"Connections to the Whole"**.

The quantum world is a network of relations, an all-encompassing and inseparable web of dynamic connections of energy and unlimited means of communication.

Although the quantum world is on an entirely different level of scale, we cannot separate it from the dynamics of the macrocosm. The microcosm is undeniably part of the macrocosm, separated only by human perceptions. Because of this all pervasive underlying unity of our physical world, it cannot and will not experience a future deadly runaway expansion, or even worse, a "ripping effect" ending in everlasting death.

The cosmic expansion has been accelerating for the last five billion years and will accelerate for much longer. However, after an appropriate length of time, our physical world will demonstrate its underlying unity **on a cosmic scale** by first reducing its accelerating expansion, then slowing down its expansion altogether until it reaches zero before embarking on a negative course of contraction.

Yes, the cyclic model of our physical world consists of two major phases: cosmic expansion which is the positive phase highlighted by its term of development, and cosmic contraction which is the negative phase. Humans evolved during the expansion phase; are they not living proof of the existence of a positive phase?!!! In between these two phases is the time that separates expansion from contraction, the period of equilibrium, neutrality and balance, an immensely important component in my philosophy of Existence in general.

Yes, on a cosmic scale, the cyclic world displays three of the most significant features, not only of nature but of Being itself:

All pervasive unity,
Rhythms of Positive and Negative
and Balance.

B.   BALANCE

Our cycle of physical existence can be compared to the life-cycle of a flower. Cosmic expansion and simultaneous development resembles the opening of a flower before full-bloom. The opening signifies the positive phase in its flowering cycle, whilst the follow-up after full-bloom, the process of aging and subsequent wilting signifies the negative phase, fully comparable to the future cosmic contraction, retrogression and death/re-formation of our physical world. In between, hopefully still to be experienced by super intelligent beings billions of years from now, will be the **"time of Full-Bloom"**, the time between ascent and descent, the time when the prevalence of development and growth comes to an end before general degeneration takes over. This beautiful upper balance (equilibrium position) of opposite phases will be the pinnacle of physical existence (although it may not necessarily include descendants from the human ancestry nor landscapes we presently experience). It will be **the era of macro-cosmic balance and age of fulfilment.**

There is irrefutable evidence of an overwhelming tendency, for the physical world in general and some of its key components in particular, in the micro as well as the macrocosm, to "seek" and "find" a harmonic balance between seemingly competing opposites and for stability and overall symmetry. Ever since the beginning of its expansion phase, our physical system was (and still is!) involved in some spectacular acts of balance. The most obvious example of a well-balanced, orderly and stable world is the impressive distribution of stars, planets, galaxies and clusters of galaxies visible in a clear sky at night. Imagine the horror if some of these bodies and system of bodies suddenly behaved erratically and flew off in different directions!

One of the most striking balancing acts occurs inside a star between the two opposite-acting forces of gravity and electro-magnetism. Gravity tries to crush the star and electro- magnetism provides the pressure to counteract. If either force would change its strength by only one part in 10^{40} (!), the following would happen:

An increase in gravity or decrease in electro-magnetism would increase the nuclear reactions in the core. Its life span would be shortened considerably and if this happened to our sun, all existing life on planet earth would come to an abrupt end. A slightly weaker gravitational pull or stronger electromagnetic force at the formation stage of a star would have prevented it to become sufficiently hot to start its nuclear reactions. Our sun and consequently our life on earth would be non-existent.

How can two seemingly competing, opposite forces inside a star be so delicately balanced as to allow it to become one of our most prominent and useful pieces of hardware in the physical world? Increasing our state of wonderment is the fact that the weak and strong forces partake in this incredibly even matched "tug of war" via controlled nuclear processes. Not only the two main players but all four forces are involved in this tightly knit and closely contested battle, an action-filled contest that, in terms of time, is ideally drawn out to allow sufficient time for the development of wonderful things on planet earth. Another outstanding act of balance in our physical system occurs inside the atom and involves the electro-magnetic force.

The atom is the smallest unit of a chemical element and consists of a nucleus surrounded by an orbiting cloud of mobile, negative charged electrons. The nucleus is composed of a ball of positive charged protons and neutral neutrons. The exception to this is the nucleus of the hydrogen atom, the lightest of all elements. It consists of only one proton and no neutrons. Because the electromagnetic force controls the structure and interactions of atoms and molecules, it is present in all matter, mostly electrically neutral, **equally balanced.**

To achieve this balance, the mass of negative charged electrons surrounding the protons and neutrons would have to be equal to the mass of the positive charged protons, which in fact it is. One electron is $1/1840$th the mass of one proton and there are 1840 electrons to every proton. The electro-magnetic force in ordinary matter is, to our knowledge, completely neutralised (balanced) throughout our physical world. The primary benefit was that it allowed sufficient time to introduce order in the early physical world and in turn initiate organic evolution and all further development on our planet.

These great examples of supreme balance and harmony may seduce us into believing that the macro-physical world has reached maturity and is now on its long way out. With the discovery of dark energy, the odds seem to be stacked against a future upper balance of opposite forces. However, **the physical world's macro activity was never and, by all accounts, will never**

be a one-way slide into oblivion. There will never be a situation of winner takes all … for ever.

Opposing forces are rearing to unleash their
power to achieve the desired objective:

Equilibrium, a time of full bloom and era of fulfilment.

The development of life throughout the physical world is still in its infancy. Barring unforeseen circumstances, an increasingly more balanced and intelligent collective human mind is (hopefully!) on its way to overcome the threats it creates for itself whilst at the same time, the creative bond between the human mind and the universal mind continues to grow. Although earth life and humans play bit parts in the overall scheme, I sincerely believe, we have the potential to break out of our cocoon of evolutionary limitations. If this happens, a more balanced and intelligent super-mind will emerge and progress to universal understanding of the nature of existence and embrace its fate of ultimate union with the universal mind. Later, cosmic contraction, degeneration, retrogression and the end of our present cycle of physical existence (before re-formation) will be understood as inevitable but necessary for the sake of not only the continued survival of our physical world, but existence as a whole.

Deeply embedded in the very structure of existence, the will to optimal survival is the most innate, all powerful and motivating agent, and to survive, the physical world most certainly will not dissolve its underlying, all pervasive unity and expand into everlasting nothingness, as it also cannot stay anchored in a state of everlasting balance.

Existence is Movement.

The only way is to return to within itself,
to recharge, re-group and re-emerge.

C.   LIMITED HUMAN KNOWLEDGE

The more we know the more we become aware how little we know!

In the not too distant past, organized systems of belief were all powerful and reigned supreme. They fed humans with all the "right" answers. They provided certainty, guidance and comfort, some underlined with threats of damnation. Humans superficially knew where they came from and where they were going.

However, nothing could stop the enquiring mind. Just when religions were at their most powerful, science threw a spanner into their works. Scientific answers replaced many traditional religious beliefs but even now, after centuries of ever improving scientific knowledge, the majority of humans still cling to an ever-increasing multitude of different religious – spiritual dogmas and persuasions of the truth. Some do it because of ignorance and others because of fear but most because science (as a matter of course) precludes moral and social values. We live in times of gradual, fundamental change and as a consequence in an era of spiritual confusion and mental turmoil. However, I am convinced that blind faith will not survive the test of time. It is a matter of great urgency that in the near future a new and competent role player must fill the ever-increasing vacuum left over by traditional religion.

In the meantime, science, with ever increasing velocity surges ahead with new theories, discoveries and ideas. Some leading physicists believed that they were well within reach of a complete theory of nature and aptly called it "The Theory of Everything" (TOE). One of the latest and most promising propositions with the potential to include all subatomic particles and forces were the superstring and brane theories. For a while they seemed to be (and for many scientists they still are) the most hopeful candidates for a "Theory of Everything!" However, mathematical obstacles and complexities are far greater than at first anticipated. There is no doubt that great strides have been made in physical science but if we dare look into the future, these past strides pale into insignificance compared to what still lies ahead. Our presently accepted views and theories are anything but safe and secure.

Just how a great scientist can be (partially!) misled by his own ideas (and prevailing circumstances) and formulate a theory without sufficient experimental or observational proof is clearly shown by Albert Einstein's declaration (before 1927) that he successfully modelled a "universe" that was held in equilibrium by the attractive force of gravity and a newly discovered cosmic repulsive force. He <u>assumed</u> that the universe was static and that the attractive force of gravity exactly matches this repulsive force. When in 1927 Edwin Hubble discovered cosmic expansion, Einstein's theory of perfect balance was rendered obsolete. His ideas were superseded by a most popular theory whereby our seemingly static physical world avoids gravitational implosion because it was supposed to be still involved in the initial big bang explosion. However, with the recent "re-discovery" of the now anything but equal repulsive force (the higher proportion of dark energy that powers the repulsive force causes the apparent acceleration of cosmic expansion) counteracting the force of gravity, Einstein's dented reputation in this regard seems to be partially restored.

The ambiguity of current cosmic expansion-contraction theories warrants consideration of all possibilities. It may be a bit unfortunate that the emphasis has now fully shifted to dark energy and dark matter. Dark energy is the buzz-word because it offered a ready explanation for the current (apparent) acceleration of cosmic expansion, although scientists actually know very little about it. Even their statement that it exists must be taken with circumspection. A beautiful and seemingly fitting explanation for everything we discover doesn't mean it is right. Considering all the hype around dark energy, it comes as a surprise that some researchers want to get rid of it entirely. They are considering a theory they call "Hubble Bubble!". The idea is that the local portion of our physical world lies in a region of space with less than average density and for this reason would expand at a faster than average rate relative to the space outside. If this was true, general cosmic expansion may be just an illusion. However, it is my humble opinion that at the present time, dark energy is the most plausible of known possibilities.

Not much is known about the true nature of dark matter, the so-called glue that binds galaxies together, counter-acting the might of dark energy. Scientists are still searching for the elusive dark matter particle although billions should be penetrating our planet as it orbits the sun. The evidence for dark matter at this stage in time remains circumstantial. Researchers also consider now an alternative theory to dark matter which they call modified gravity theory. The idea is that over distances of millions of light years, gravity behaves differently.

Regards critical density value miscalculation, the major factor that could lead to possible faulty information is the origin of the critical density value.

This depends to a large extent on Hubble's constant H that determines how fast the physical world is expanding. To this day there is still no consent among scientists as to its exact value. The constant H is also used to calculate the volume of the physical world which in turn is the main component in calculating the actual density value.

In view of all the uncertainties still associated with cosmic expansion, contraction and the end of our cycle of physical existence, isn't it possible that a hereto unknown major element or system could still change our whole perspective on the above? It may border on science-fiction but if we consider "whole universe symmetry" and take into account the existence of an anti-matter world, the whole scenario of overall dynamics and the end of our cycle, would fundamentally change.

Assuming that our partner-world expands in similar ways to ours and they both are on a space-geometric course that ultimately would bring them into each other's field of forces and energy, the most likely outcome would be first a remarkable expansion slow down, then a moment of cosmic equilibrium followed by a rapid increase of combined gravitational contraction and later, in a spectacular show of physical destruction, the annihilation of all energy including radiation. The big crunch would, for the most minute length of ordinary time, end in a transubstantiation from particles of energy into Potentia, leaving no trace of our physical world. The re-formation would be accomplished via a quantum fluctuation according to the inflation theory. The probability of above scenario is small because science tells us that no initial mixture of matter and anti-matter could develop into separate worlds without first annihilating itself. However, our knowledge of astrophysics and the "Beyond" is still in its infancy and therefore extremely

limited .....

THE CYCLIC MODEL

There was no "toss-up" in my choice between the cyclic model and the presently still more popular standard model, the once-off trajectory from creation to annihilation (from the big bang to the long slow death by expansion or, alternatively, to a last big crunch).

Why did I finally choose the cyclic model as the most likely version of physical existence on a cosmic scale? Not because cycles are the most expressive and prominent changes in nature and not only because cycles incorporate an explicit element of positive and negative states, qualities and characteristics. Apart from the reasons presented before, I finally choose the cyclic model because, from my point of view, it deeply reflects the true essence of nature:

Constant Activity – Movement and Change.

The activity is endless, the physical world undergoes endless cycles of cosmic expansion and contraction, each beginning with a big bang and ending in a big crunch. Unceasing cosmic activity is guaranteed by the physical world's interdependence with the U-Minded world. Unimpeded by the space-time limitations of our physical system, the U-Mind is set on only one "vision":

Optimal Existence and Continuity thereof.

Physical Existence is not a limited time event. The inherent effects of the principle of existence not only suggest but emphasise lasting activity (movements). In my view there is no evidence of cessation because the Universal Mind is set in a realm free of ordinary space-time limitations, and what is grounded in the realm of no future and no past but an eternally moving present, will never cease to exist.

The alternative to the cyclic model is the standard big bang theory. In its conventional form, it is **a Journey from Nothing to Nothing.**

NOTHING VERSUS EXISTENCE

Nothing can come out of nothing!

This is what humankind believed for thousands of years. During the later part of the twentieth century, physicists and cosmologists began to tell us that "everything" came out of nothing!

It is generally accepted that the physical world started off with the big bang. A plausible scientific explanation for the conventional big bang was (and to a great extent still is) the inflation theory by Alan Guth in 1980 combined with the grand unified theories (GUT's). The first GUT was published in 1973 by Sheldon Glashow and Howard Georgi. Combined, the theories in effect state that the physical world spontaneously burst out of - nothing. Tiny bubbles of empty space (quantum fluctuations) began to inflate at an accelerating rate, consequently creating an unstable "false" vacuum with huge negative pressure infused with incredible amounts of "self-created" energy (virtual particles of very brief existence). The estimated size of this early "universe" was approximately one billionth the radius of a proton! Due to its unstable nature, the false vacuum began to decay, the inflation ceased and the negative pressure disappeared but the colossal amount of created energy suddenly transformed into this intensely hot fireball that we now commonly refer to as the big bang.

This, in short, was (and mostly still is) one of the most acceptable of several scientific theories of the beginning of our physical world.

It is also the basic tenet of creation "ex Nihilo" in its modern quantum mechanical form.

The so-called "universe" erupted spontaneously out of nothing!

What is nothing?

Nothing is the non-existent.

A rational way to express "nothing" is by means of the mathematical symbol "zero", indicating the absence of any quantity.

The word zero comes from the Arabic language and is a translation of a Hindu word meaning "empty" or "void". The concept of zero can be traced back to Hindu mathematicians of about 300 B.C. (considering its meaning, the addition of zeros to the nine other Arabic numerals in order to write any number, however large, seems to be quite paradoxical). Mathematics is the language of science and nature and the digit zero holds a unique place in all mathematical calculations. Zero as an expression of quantity is exactly what it means: Nothing, empty and void. Why then does science suggest that "everything" came out of nothing?

It is impossible because in the context of universality, "Nothing" is "Negation of Existence", the absence of anything. One possible explanation is that they refer to "things" they <u>know</u> that exist. The familiar world of humans is based on what they see, hear, smell, taste and touch and anything else is supposedly built on logic and sound reasoning. However, whilst appreciating the incredible development of the human mind, we ought to, at all times, be fully aware of our limits of knowledge. Why didn't they just state that the physical world emerged from the unknown?

Before the grand unified theories were applied to explain the early expansion of the physical world, scientists used Einstein's theory of gravity and general relativity to follow the present expansion back in time to a single point of zero size. However, according to the theory of general relativity, this zero point was also supposed to accommodate all matter and energy of the so-called universe at …… infinite density, temperature and strength of gravity! This unavoidable situation is a particularly bad example of the dreaded infinity disease that pesters many theories in physics. It is named a "singularity". To avoid being consumed by such a "singularity", the scientists smeared it out with the help of the quantum theory in which uncertainty is a central tenet. Applying the uncertainty principle would create the unique situation of **finite extent in space without a starting point.**

The question of "What happened at or before the beginning of the physical world" would then, in their opinion, become meaningless because of the foamy and frothlike structure of space-time on the quantum scale. Unfortunately, a full and satisfactory quantum theory of gravity does not exist and therefore many scientific key questions concerning the mysteries of cosmic expansion (and contraction) remain unanswered. A future version of super string or brane theory may still prove to give sensible physical results (that adequately fit all the facts of nature) but such a theory is still incomplete without a satisfactory explanation of the basic physical and metaphysical principles that lead to its structure.

My theory of the beginning of the present cycle of physical existence is based on logical considerations and structured on the inevitable conclusion, **that the totality of our physical world could never have begun to exist from absolute nothing.**

I reject the view of some prominent physicists that the physical world may have been the "ultimate free lunch".

It is a short sighted view and based entirely on present limitations of scientific knowledge. What popular physical science and, from a different point of view, some religions inferred to be the beginning or "creation" of "the universe" was in fact the emergence of a new cycle, **the "re-formation" of the physical mode of existence.**

Comparable to a day's end and a new day's beginning at midnight, the previous cycle of physical existence ended at the last moment of time X whilst the present cycle began at the first instant, also of time X. The traditional "moment of creation" or the fashionable "time zero" some physicists refer to, has become obsolete.

The main reason why some physicists still regard **the physical state re-formation** a first time/one-time event is the fact that most of their conclusions are based on superficial macro and micro-cosmic evidence.

3

MOVEMENTS – FORCES AND ENERGY

MATTER

MOLECULES AND ATOMS

At its most basic level, all matter is movement!

But how can solid matter, the likes of wood or steel basically just be movement?

Scientists, plunging ever deeper into matter discovered that most material things consist of molecules, the smallest recognizable parts of a chemical compound and therefore the smallest possible portion of a material substance (either a solid, liquid or gas). They are found on a microscopic level where "things" are becoming a bit hazy and common sense ideas about the nature of matter are starting to break down. A glass of water for example contains many molecules of the compound water. Each molecule of water consists of two hydrogen atoms chemically combined with one oxygen atom. As can be seen, a molecule is a combination of two or more atoms held together by cohesive electrical forces and ... horror of all horrors, **molecules are in constant dancing motion!**

The state of a material substance as a solid, liquid or gas depends upon the concentration and mobility of its molecules. In solids, molecules are tightly packed together. In ice for example, molecules do move, however, their movement is very limited. As we add energy to ice in the form of heat radiation, we increase the amount of movement of each molecule. The molecules slowly separate from each other and form a liquid state. Unlike the solid state where the individual molecules are relatively fixed in place, molecules of the compound water can now easily move past one another and the dancing becomes freer and quicker. As we add even more heat to the sample, the molecules separate further until the point at which there is relatively little interaction between them. At this point, the individual molecules move very quickly. This is called the gas state. In water, the gas state is achieved by boiling water to form steam.

A dancing molecule is a combination of at least two or more atoms and this raises the question: What is an atom?

The atom is the (smallest) unit of a chemical element and curiously enough, consists almost entirely of empty space. It has a nucleus of positively charged particles, protons and electrically neutral neutrons (with the exception of the lightest chemical element hydrogen which has one proton and no neutron) and, matching in mass and opposite charge, one negatively charged electron per proton swirling cloudlike around the nucleus. Every atom, each corresponding to the modern version of a chemical element, is different from another and always electrically neutral (balanced). The difference depends on the number of protons (and matching neutrons and electrons) which is equal to the atomic number and determines the chemical properties of an element. The heavy chemical element Uranium for examples has an atomic number of 92.

The atom is transformed by nuclear reactions and remains unchanged during chemical change. The forces controlling the nucleus and electrons are electrical (electromagnetic force) in nature whilst the nuclear force holds the particles of the nucleus, the protons, neutrons and quarks (inside them!) together. To scale, the human is to an atom what a star is to us. Although we can see neither electrons nor the nucleus and cannot accurately picture the structure of an atom, sensitive microscopes with a magnification in millions reveal that within the dancing molecule, **atoms are in constant motion!**

MATTER PARTICLES

Subatomic matter particles are unlike marbles. They are fuzzy and ghostlike, bound to one another by forces. These forces are carried from particle to particle by even more ethereal entities.

This, more or less, is the image we have of subatomic particles. However, matter particles in motion display another important feature.

It all started in the early 1920's. While physicists were still trying in pain to explain the wave-particle duality of light, a French aristocrat and physicist Prince Louis de Broglie dropped a bomb shell. He came up with the idea that particles of matter in motion could also have wave-like features. In 1925 he arrived at a formula that enabled the "wave length" associated with a particle to be calculated. Experimental evidence for matter waves emerged in 1927 when Clinton Davisson, an American physicist discovered that it was possible to form an interference pattern by beaming electrons onto a crystal surface. This could only be explained if electrons were waves. Now physicists not only had to try to explain the wave-particle duality of radiation, but also the particle-wave duality of matter. Depending on the type of experiment, matter can either reveal the marble-like characteristic of particles (as in collisions and scattering experiments), or their wave-like property.

At about the same time (1926), Erwin Schrödinger published his famous wave equation. It revealed that matter waves are anything but real waves. To reflect the abstract nature of these so-called waves, he dubbed them wave functions but still visualised particles of matter as a kind of real "standing" waves. In his formula, the wave function enshrines mathematically the wave-like behaviour of a particle but doesn't say anything about the wave itself. The formula was an unquestionable success. It was able to deal with complex problems posed by atoms with more than one set of electrons which Bohr's theory was unable to solve.

We know that a matter particle, whilst moving along a pre-set path from A to B, is able to be "everywhere" (within limits) at once. A subatomic particle does not follow a precise trajectory at all. Its motion is fuzzy-wavy. It seems to "feel out" all possible paths simultaneously. These paths contribute to the total wave that represents the particle. The degree to which a particle "feels" its way from the straight line is determined by its mass. A heavier particle keeps more to the straight line. The phenomenon can easily be demonstrated by means of the double slit experiment, using electrons instead of particles of light.

Although "structural" details are lost in the fuzziness of quantum uncertainty, we know from experiments that subatomic particles have certain properties such as mass-energy, either positive, negative or neutral electric charge and a kind of mysterious, intrinsic spin. Spin is a property inherent in nearly all subatomic particles but most evident in electrons and quarks, the main-constituents of matter. Doesn't this tell us something?

My theory of quantum particles unequivocally states that what we define as an elementary particle is not a "thing" in the usual sense and nothing material but movements of an abstract entity and the restmass-energy of an elementary particle of matter is inseparably connected to **movements within (contained).**

Details of elementary particle movements are highly speculative. The property of spin as noted by scientists is the result of their interaction (with the particle) and not a true reflection of its actual movement within. In my view, spin is most probably vortex-like but unlike that of a whirlpool or cyclone, it is "spherical" for particles with mass and less so for particles with little and flat for particles with no mass, fully in accord with the strangeness of the quantum world in general. It is a kind of "clock or anticlock-wise inward, standing spin" towards a centre point corresponding to positive or negative electric charge respectively. It is not my intention to force-fit the movement of an abstract-existent entity into an everyday frame work of common sense idea. However, I find it challenging to try to forward the most possible and likely concept by means of the power of imagination.

Some matter particles with neutral charge contain elementary particles that induce cancelation, for example the neutron consists of two "down" quarks of $\frac{1}{3}$ of a unit negative electric charge each and one "up" quark of $\frac{2}{3}$ of a unit positive electric charge.

A proton consists of two "up" quarks of $\frac{2}{3}$ of a unit positive electric charge each and a "down" quark of $\frac{1}{3}$ of a unit negative electric charge, making up a net positive charge of 1 unit. Some elementary particles, such as neutrinos may also have intrinsic charge cancellation facilities.

In Paragraph 5 I stated that the nature of a subatomic, elementary particle is "two sided"*. Its bewildering physical aspect is well known but its deep inner

---

*   Not to be confused with the wave-particle duality.

aspect, hidden beyond ordinary space and time in the realm of the U-Minded world, is almost unknown. By modelling a scientifically structureless matter entity along the lines of "spherical" **vortex-like movement,**[*]

we may be able to solve three problems at once. Firstly, it obliterates the "infinite energy source" problem of a pointlike particle (which gave rise to the dreaded infinity disease that affected quantum energy calculations before re-normalization was introduced).

Secondly, the theory that prevented tiny ball like particles to exist does not apply to our model because subatomic particles (movement-energy) do not consist of any ordinary material-physical substance. A raw state particle is an abstract-existent entity and because it is constantly under the influence of Potentia-partis, all "regions" of the entity respond to impact immediately (faster than the speed of light!).

Thirdly, it helps us understand the before-mentioned two-sided nature of elementary particles. The vortex-like particle movement may be contained whirling movement toward a centre point. The movement-energy and forces increase toward the point and at a critically high level of energy, **transmutation** of movement-energy to Potentia-partis occurs. The problem of infinite energy at the centre of a single point will be avoided and the mystery of the two-sided nature of a particle solved. Heavier particles have intrinsic spherical inward movements whilst light particles moving at or close to the speed of light have flattened, still vortex-like movements to induce transmutation.

The elementary particles of matter are:

a) Electron, muon, tau.
b) Electron neutrino, muon neutrino, tau neutrino.
c) Quarks: up, charm, top
                       down, strange, bottom

All quarks carry fractional, either positive or negative electric charge. They all come in three different varieties (red, blue and green) and each of those in two

---

[*]   The Higgs Boson particle may be equipped with a vortex-like movement distribution facility. It is suggested that the Higgs Boson stuck to mass-less particles shortly after the big bang, thereby creating all particles of matter.

different types of spin. In addition, for every quark of each colour and spin, there exists an anti-quark.

It is an interesting fact that all ordinary matter is made up of the two lightest quarks (up and down) and the two lightest leptons, the electron and its neutrino.

ELECTROMAGNETIC RADIATION

Electromagnetic radiation is the emission of electromagnetic energy in the form of waves or, when considered in small quantities, as particles called photons. All electromagnetic radiation is movement and movement is an act or process indicating a change of position or place. In the macrocosm the favoured line of movement from A to B of most objects is a straight line or the line of least resistance. The same can be said of electromagnetic rays, for example light rays, they also behave in such a way as to minimise their total activity. However, rays consist of radiation energy, waves or particles that never follow a straight line.

WAVES

In 1865, James Clerk Maxwell predicted that it is possible to disturb an electromagnetic field and create waves that travel through space. For example, if electrons move toward the nucleus of an atom, they are slowed down by the interaction of their electric charge with the electromagnetic force field surrounding the nucleus. The kinetic energy (energy of motion) lost by the electrons is transformed into radiant energy or electromagnetic radiation. Maxwell proclaimed that electro magnetic actions are transverse waves of energy travelling at a fixed speed through space, similar to and equal to the speed of light. In fact, an electromagnetic wave behaves like a water-wave (undulating in the two dimensions perpendicular to their direction of motion) but is of a rather complex nature. Along any wave, electric and magnetic fields **vibrate** at right angles, both to each other and to the direction of motion of the wave as shown on **Figure 1.**

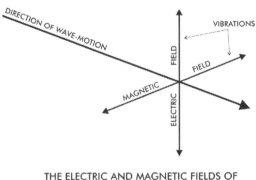

THE ELECTRIC AND MAGNETIC FIELDS OF
AN ELECTRO-MAGNETIC RADIATION WAVE

FIGURE 1.

Wavelengths vary from less than a fifty billionth of a millimetre for those radiations produced by cosmic rays, to thousands of kilometres for waves produced by alternating current.

The length of each wave times the number of waves passing a given point per second (frequency) is equal to the velocity of the electromagnetic waves which is constant at about 300,000 Km per second. Since the velocity is constant, the frequency increases as the wave length decreases; as the frequency increases, the energy also increases. Thus, the shorter the wave length of the radiation, the greater the energy.

Electromagnetic radiation for infrared, visible light, ultra violet and x-radiation are formed when an electron moving towards the nucleus of an atom is slowed by the interaction of the electric charge of the electron and the electric field surrounding the nucleus.

The kinetic energy lost by the electron is transformed into photons (or waves) of radiant energy (radiation).* The higher the initial velocity of the electron toward the nucleus, the higher the frequency of the radiation and consequently the higher the energy. If the electron for example comes from a cyclotron, very high frequency X-rays are emitted. If it comes from the electron-gun in a television picture tube, visible light is radiated. The wave lengths of visible light range from approximately 3800 to 7600 angstroms (100,000,000 angstroms equals 1 centimetre). Ultraviolet radiation is a type of invisible radiation that has wave lengths shorter than those of visible light (from 136 to 4,000 angstroms). The most common source of U.V. radiation is sunlight.

Wave lengths of X-rays extend from approximately 0.04 to 500 angstrom units. It is a penetrating form of electromagnetic radiation and can more easily pass through spaces between molecules in matter. This characteristic gives X-rays

---

* The two most useful forms of electromagnetic energy, electricity and electromagnetic radiation can be found in and near the same wire respectively through which a current (dynamic electricity) in the form of exited electrons is moving. If manmade or other obstructions are present in the wire, the atoms get in the way of the moving electrons, the electrons are slowed down and their loss of kinetic energy is transferred into waves (or photons) of electromagnetic radiation, for example heat (energy) or light (energy) as in toasters and light bulbs.

wide use in examining the interiors of almost anything from welded joints in steel plates to living organisms.

Gamma rays are electromagnetic radiations of very short wavelength emitted by certain radioactive elements. They have enormous powers of penetration and because of their extremely high frequency and energy content are used in cancer treatment and diagnostic applications.

At the end of the scale are the cosmic rays. They have the shortest wavelengths, are extremely penetrating and reach our planet from all directions in space.

Infrared radiation (heat radiation) has longer wave lengths than those of visible light. This type of radiation is invisible to the eye and occurs primarily from objects heated to high temperatures. It is generated by the vibrations of the molecules making up the object. Infrared wave lengths range from approximately 0.76 micron, bordering visible red light, to about 300 microns, close to the limit of radio waves used for radar.

The length of radio waves range from about 1 centimetre to approximately 10 kilometres and the longest electromagnetic radiation waves are the alternating current waves produced by electric generators. Their lengths can reach thousands of kilometres.

PARTICLES

The concept of a particle of light was introduced by the German physicist Max Planck in 1900 whilst trying to solve the "Problem of contradiction" between Maxwell's wave theory of light and the classical theory of heat.

He found that he could only solve the problem by assuming that light was not a continuous wave but comes in discrete packets of energy (quanta). This was a radical and seemingly absurd assumption as light was thought of as being wavelike.

In 1905 Einstein verified Planck's "Hypothesis of Quanta". He demonstrated that light is particlelike by using the photoelectric effect.

The dual nature (wave-particle) of electromagnetic radiation was finally demonstrated and proved beyond any doubt in 1923 by the American physicist Arthur Compton in his famous scattering experiment. He fired X-rays (waves) onto a thin metal plate and to everybody's surprise some of the X-rays bounced off the electrons in the plate **as if they were particles.**

Some went straight through while others were only slightly deflected. Compton measured the frequencies of the X-rays before and after the collision. The frequencies of those X-rays that were involved in head-on collisions with the electrons were noticeably lower, having passed on some of their energy to the electrons. The energy loss confirmed Planck's formula $E = hf$. The particle of electromagnetic radiation was named **Photon** (Greek: phos, photos, light).

Every photon has electric and magnetic vibrations orientated at right angles both to each other and to the direction of motion of the photon as shown on **Figure 2.**

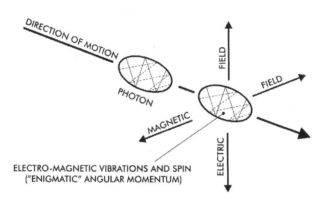

ELECTRO-MAGNETIC VIBRATIONS AND SPIN
("ENIGMATIC" ANGULAR MOMENTUM)

THE ELECTRIC AND MAGNETIC FIELDS OF PHOTONS

FIGURE 2.

The photon is considered to be the fundamental and indivisible energy particle or quantum of visible light and other electromagnetic radiation. It has no rest-mass and derives its energy from its motion (kinetic energy) proportional to the frequency of the radiation and thus inversely proportional to the wavelength of the radiation. Each photon of a given colour of light for example has a certain amount of energy. Reducing the intensity of a beam of red light only reduces the number of photons in the beam, however, each remaining photon still has the same amount of energy as any other photon of red light. High frequency violet light is made of higher energy photons than the low frequency red light. The higher the radiation frequency, the higher the energy of the photons.

The physicist can never accurately determine the paths of individual photons, however, he can calculate the probability of finding "it" in a given place of impact provided that the experiment has been properly prepared.

When a photon is created, it travels instantly at the speed of light. It is impossible for it to slow down nor can it be slowed down because it has no rest-mass to slow it and it is impossible for it to speed up because nothing can travel faster than the speed of light. It has no electric charge but like most other particles, it has the mysterious characteristic of spin. Spin is such a fundamental characteristic of a particle that any alteration in the rate of spin would either destroy it or change it fundamentally. Spin is calculated in terms of angular momentum and is based upon Planck's constant. Because the angular momentum is so small, physicists indicate the spin of other subatomic particles by relating it to the spin of a photon which is 1. For example particles of the family of fermions have either spin $\frac{1}{2}$ or $\frac{3}{2}$ (protons, electrons and neutrons have spin $\frac{1}{2}$) and particles of the family of bosons have either spin 0 (the Higgs particle), 1 (Photon, W & Z particles) or 2 (graviton). The spin behaviour of bosons is extremely abstruse and appeals to intuition. The huge gap between particles of the fermion family and the ones of the boson family exists because physicists associate the fermions with matter and the bosons with forces. Yes, according to physicists, our particle under discussion is not only the "quantum" of electromagnetic radiation (a fully-fledged particle with infinite life span), but as virtual particle with extremely short life span, it plays the part of force-carrier of the electromagnetic force (electro-magnetism) where it controls the structure and interactions of atoms and molecules.

It has to be mentioned that spin as stated by physicists is the result of their interaction with the particle and does not reflect actual movement which I think in the case of bosons is fairly flat vortex- like.

FORCES

Most of the information in this section is in accordance with the standard physics text book.

For my ideas on the dynamic source of forces and force fields see "Movements and Forces".

A force changes or tends to change the state of motion or rest of a body. In nature, any cause which changes or tends to change the (apparent!) rest or direction or speed of motion of a part of matter or radiation (starlight can be deflected by the gravitational forcefield of the sun!), is called a force. Four fundamental forces of nature have so far been identified:

Gravity
Electromagnetism
Weak Nuclear Force and
Strong Nuclear Force

With the exception of intrinsic contained particle movements, fundamentally, these forces account for all of nature's random, interconnected and organised activity. As different types of "glue" they are main components in building a world of optimal complexity. If there was an absence of forces, elementary particles of matter would simply move about in a featureless world (in my scheme, particles could not exist without their forces, as movement – energy, charge and forces are intrinsic, interconnected properties).

Organised activity is abundantly made clear by the fact that forces are protected by conservation laws, the stronger the force, the more restrictions are imposed, for example the strong nuclear force is restricted (and therefore protected) by the full compliment of twelve conservation laws, the electromagnetic force by eleven, the weak by eight but gravity has not been fully researched as yet.

The four basic forces are thought to have originated from a single super force that existed momentarily during the big bang. It would have contained all the ingredients for the creation of the four forces, but in my view, the super-force so vehemently sought after by theoretical physicists was only a means to an end. It was the symmetry breaking that was ingenious because the resultant four forces now hold the physical world together as a dynamic, harmonious and well balanced entity. The separation itself is a reflection of the staggering, single minded "genius "displayed by the U-Mind.

Force requires energy. Every force is associated with a force-carrying particle. The electric and magnetic forces with the photon, the strong nuclear force with the gluon, the weak nuclear force with the "W" and "Z" boson and the force of gravity with the graviton. Gravity and electro-magnetism are familiar in everyday life. By contrast, the strong and weak nuclear forces are active only on subatomic levels.

Each type of force is transmitted through a force-field consisting of above mentioned force-carrier particle. A force field has a strength and a direction at each point in space. The strength determines the magnitude of the force exerted and the direction tells you which way the force pushes. Let us have a closer look at each force:

GRAVITY

According to physics, gravity, a property of matter, is the natural attraction between all bodies. It is the most universal of all four forces and next to the dark energy it is the main player in our physical system. In keeping the physical world together, it gallantly opposes the dark energy which presently, with considerable success, drives it apart. Although the force gets weaker with increasing distance between cosmic matter, its force-fields extend through-out space. The other three forces only affect a certain type of particle or have a very limited range. Nothing in the physical world escapes its grip, even starlight can be deflected by our sun's gravitational force. Without gravity there would be no earth, sun, galaxies or even a physical world.

Sir Isaac Newton formulated the law of gravitation which was published in 1687. Newton's law was unchallenged until Albert Einstein in 1915 created his general theory of relativity. According to Einstein, gravity is essentially a curving or warping of space and time (space cannot only stretch and shrink, it can also bend and distort). Over time, sensitive tests of his theory of gravity were devised and they all have been passed with flying colours (Newton's theory remains satisfactory for most practical purposes such as aircraft navigation and most astronomical systems). It was only until they tried to treat gravity as just another quantum field that things began to fail. It seemed impossible to create quantum gravity out of Einstein's theory of general relativity. However, most scientists decided to carry on as if gravity is just another quantum field. The theory of superstrings, according to some scientists the greatest step forward to a super theory of nature, apparently demands that the graviton (the particle of gravity) exists. Presently we have this unique situation of two different interpretations for the same force. A proper understanding of gravity (and the newly discovered dark energy) would be the key to unlock the mysteries of our cosmos.

Gravity can best be described as a field. According to most physicists, every particle of matter is the source of a gravitational field surrounding it with an invisible halo of influence. On the quantum scale it is extremely feeble (it is the most feeble of all four forces, only 10^{-39} of the electromagnetic force between the electron and the nucleus of a hydrogen atom and 10^{32} times weaker than the weak nuclear force). However, the force of gravity accumulates as more and more matter accumulates. On a large scale, a gigantic field unleashes a tremendous force exemplified by the existence of black holes.

Waves can be set up in the gravitational field that travel through space. These waves are like ripples of space itself, however, they carry energy (momentum) but physically they are just undulating emptiness. The still hypothetical (there is no concrete proof of their existence) particles of gravity waves and force fields are called gravitons. Just like the photons of electromagnetic waves and fields, gravitons travel at the speed of light, have zero rest-mass and are neutrally charged. However, they have two units of spin instead of the one unit of photons. As full fledged (just like the photons, gravitons come in two varieties: full fledged and virtual) force carriers speeding back and forth, they keep the planets in their orbits and bind you and me to the ground. Their life span is infinite.

On the quantum level, when two subatomic particles of matter exert a gravitational influence on each other, virtual (having only a temporary, fleeting existence) gravitons convey an extremely feeble attractive force from particle to particle. These virtual gravitons are (theoretically) accountable for the existence of every subatomic matter particle's extremely weak gravitational field, mainly "along- side" the very much stronger electromagnetic and nuclear force fields within atoms and molecules.

ELECTRO-MAGNETISM

Electro-magnetism is the term given to magnetic forces produced by electricity. A simple but good example of electro-magnetism is when you pick up a piece of paper with a plastic comb after combing your hair. The induced charge to the otherwise static electricity of the comb produced the "magnetic" force required to pick up the paper.

To help dispel confusion regards the terms electricity, magnetism and electro-magnetism let us have a quick look at the different but interrelated phenomena of electricity and magnetism:

Electricity is the manifestation of a form of energy resulting from the existence of charged particles, either statically as an accumulation of charge or dynamically as a current of electricity.

Electricity is present in all matter as positively charged protons and negatively charged electrons. In most bodies there are equal numbers of each so that the body is electrically neutral and no phenomenon is observed. This is static electricity or electricity at rest. Current or dynamic electricity is the form that has become immensely useful to humans. It is mainly produced by generators in power-stations.

Induction is the electrification by proximity to a highly charged body or a body through which a current is passing. Induced electrification is always opposite to that of a source.

"Electric forces" come in two varieties, either as a positive charge or a negative charge. Like electric charges repel, unlike electric charges attract, some particles are electrically neutral.

Magnetism is the property by means of which certain objects called magnets can exert mechanical force on nearby objects of suitable composition without the need for any direct or indirect physical contact.

Natural magnets or lodestones, made from the complex iron-oxide ore called magnetite ($Fe^3 O^4$) have for thousands of years been known to attract iron.

An object made of a ferro-magnetic material, when placed in a magnetic field, acquires the properties of a magnet. This process is called magnetic induction.

A magnetic field is any region throughout which the magnetizing force of a magnet exerts its influence. The path which a freely moving north pole would follow in a magnetic field is called a line of force. Early voyages of discovery made use of the principle of steel magnets freely supported by a string. One end of the magnet pointed nearly north and the other nearly south. The steel magnets were made by stroking the metal with a lodestone or another magnet.

An ordinary bar magnet possesses a north pole and a south pole, however, a deeper analysis reveals that magnetism is **actually produced by electric currents circulating at the atomic level.**

This, quite clearly, shows the interrelationship between magnetism and electricity. There is no such thing as "pure" magnetism. Inside every magnet a loop of electric current inevitably produces a pair of magnetic poles, a north and a south pole. Magnetic poles always come in pairs, it is impossible to cut a single pole out of a bar magnet. Like magnetic poles repel, unlike poles attract. Magnetism is always associated with moving electrical charges present in an electric current and can also uniquely induce an electric voltage or potential in any nearby electrical conductor, provided that conductor is moving relative to the source of the magnetism.

The strength of the electric and magnetic forces diminish with distance according to the same "inverse square" law that Newton deduced for gravity. This brings us back to the abstract concept of field. As with gravity the effects of electric and magnetic forces can best be understood in terms of a field, a sort of invisible halo of influence emanating from matter and extending through space (the magnetic field of the earth extends far out into space).

The Greek philosopher Thales (born in 640 B.C.), also called the father of philosophy, is credited with the first definite identification of electricity. He discovered that if he rubbed amber (a fossil resin) with a cloth, he was able to pick up small pieces of metal (the word Elektron is Greek for Amber). Natural magnetism (found in lodestones) was also identified at about the same time by the early Greeks.

The connection between electricity and magnetism was discovered in the early nineteenth century. Hans Christian Oersted, a Danish physicist, is regarded as the father of electro-magnetism. In the early 1800's he discovered that a magnetic needle turns at right angles to an electric current, meaning that the electric current actually generates a magnetic field around itself.

In 1821 Michael Faraday, an English scientist discovered that the rotation of a magnetic pole induced an electric current to flow. These discoveries led to the invention of the dynamo and the generator.

In the 1850's James Clerk Maxwell brought together mathematically the electric and magnetic fields in creating magnetism by means of a varying electric field. It unified electricity and magnetism into a single electromagnetic field. Maxwell's equations made up the first unified field theory.

Without electro-magnetism there would be no atoms, molecules and no solid, liquid and gaseous matter as we know.

On the quantum level when, for example, two negatively charged electrons come close together, they experience an electric repulsive force and rush off in different directions. The electrons don't touch each other, the electromagnetic field that emanates from each electron prevents this from happening.

A force requires energy. Although the electromagnetic field of each electron has a strength and direction at each point in space, the energy coming from each electron is transmitted through the field in small packets or quanta. These are the force-carrying particles called photons. The photon with one unit of spin, has no rest-mass and no electric charge but derives its energy from its motion. However, as force carrier on the quantum level, the photon is not a full fledged particle with infinite lifespan. In this particular role it is a rather ephemeral entity, a so-called virtual particle that exists on "borrowed" energy for a fleeting moment. The electron, like all electrically charged particles, is constantly emitting and re-absorbing virtual photons in superfast time so as not to violate the conservation law of mass-energy. If two electrons come so close together that their virtual photon-cloud overlaps, it is possible that virtual photons emitted from one electron are absorbed by the other and vice-versa. The repulsive force between them is the effect of the mutual exchange (also called interaction) of virtual photons. The same happens but with opposite effect when an electron with negative electric charge meets a proton with positive charge. In this case there is mutual attraction whilst two protons again repulse each other.

Force carrying photons may only live for a fleeting moment but as a cloud of virtual photons they fulfil one of the most important roles in the micro-physical system: they control the structure and interactions of atoms and molecules.

WEAK NUCLEAR FORCE

The weak nuclear force accounts for one of the three types of radioactivity, the so-called beta-decay (the break-up of neutrons in the nuclei of certain atoms).

It all began in 1896. Henri Becquerel, a French physicist was doing some research into the phenomenon of phosphorescence when he accidentally discovered radio-activity. In early March, he developed some photographic plates that had been left unattended for several days in the cupboard next to some uranium crystals. It was the mysterious fogging of these plates that baffled him. Kept in the dark cupboard for so long, the uranium crystals should have lost their ability to fog the plates. It dawned on him that the crystals are emitting rays of something else than just phosphorescence. Becquerel, in his quest to solve the mysteries of glowing compounds had just discovered an important new property of matter – Radioactivity.

Research into radioactive emission was slow at first. A systematic study was undertaken by the English physicist Ernest Rutherford and the chemist Frederick Soddy in the early twentieth century. They finally characterised the three types of radiation. The first kind was called Alpha Radiation. The heavy, positively charged particles of alpha radiation turned out to be fast-moving helium nuclei made up of two protons and two neutrons. But it was the second type[*], beta radiation that puzzled scientists and the more they learned about it, the stranger it seemed. The first discovery was that radioactivity involved the gradual loss of mass (decay) of the material involved. In the beta type of radioactivity it emerged that it was the nuclei of the atoms themselves that were decaying. The second discovery was that the beta particles were shown to be high speed electrons. But how can electrons emanate from the nucleus of atoms, they are supposed to be in orbit around it and not inside it as well? Most disturbing was the fact that the speed of the electrons coming out of the nucleus could not account for the total amount of the energy involved

---

[*] The third was gamma radiation.

in the decay. Some of the energy seemed to be missing. It appeared that the law of energy conservation was being violated. In 1931 the Austrian physicist Wolfgang Pauli proposed that the law of energy conservation is still true, it is just that with beta decay some of the unaccounted energy must be in the form of yet another new unseen particle. It had to have no charge and had to be intensely penetrating (cannot have much interaction with ordinary matter) – hence its elusiveness. The Italian physicist Enrico Fermi named the new, as yet undiscovered particle the "neutrino", meaning little neutral one. Neutrinos turned out to be so elusive that they were not definitely spotted until 1956, more than twenty years after Pauli's prediction.

The mystery of how electrons and the unseen particles were able to emerge from the nuclei of atoms was finally solved by Enrico Fermi. In the early 1930's he claimed that the electrons and neutrinos did not exist prior to their high speed ejection but that the neutrons in the nucleus of specific atoms were being **forced** to turn into other particles: electrons, protons and neutrinos (anti- neutrinos). Confirmation was received when physicists discovered that a "freed" neutron, isolated in the laboratory, decays (it is rather a transmutation by force) after several minutes, leaving behind a proton, electrons and anti- neutrinos. It started to dawn on physicists that known forces could not act on a neutron that way. Theoretical work proved that the newly discovered force of nature was incredibly weak, much weaker than electromagnetism (the force that holds the electrons in orbit around the nucleus), although still much stronger than gravity. Fermi's force was dubbed the weak nuclear interaction (force). After the discovery of isolated neutron decay, scientists found that the weak force was responsible for other transmutations, for example changing the flavour of quarks. The weak force does not exert a push or pull in the mechanical engineering sense with the exception of supernova explosions. By forcing transmutation in the identity of particles, it is quite different in character from either the gravitational force or electro-magnetism.

The influence of the weak nuclear force is limited to an extremely small region of space. Only since the 1980's have scientists been able to measure its range with any sort of accuracy. In general, the weak force is not operational beyond a range of about 10^{-16} cm of its source, absolutely confined to individual subatomic particles.

It was in the mid 1930's that Hideki Yukawa, a Japanese physician gave birth to the idea that all forces are ultimately the result of special force-carrying particles. In 1938 he predicted the properties of a new force-carrier for the weak nuclear force, the W-particle. It was a boson just like the photon of electro-magnetism with one unit of spin. This gave rise to the question: Was there a deeper relationship between the unlikely forces of electro-magnetism and the weak nuclear force? It transpired that there had to be another force-carrying particle to bring the two forces together. In 1961, Sheldon Glashow of Harvard University published the theory for the additional force-carrier and named it the Z° particle. However, his theory implied that just like the photon, the W and Z particles had no mass. This was a major flaw. Because of its short range, the weak force has to have force-carriers which have a large rest-mass. As virtual particles their energy is borrowed and because of their large mass the rules of the uncertainty principle demand that the loan has to be repaid within an extremely short time (about 10^{-26}s).

A schoolmate and fellow theorist of Glashow's, Steven Weinberg and the Pakistani Abdus Salam of Imperial College, London worked independently trying to overcome the problem of the two massless particles. They made use of an idea put forward by Peter Higgs of the University of Edinburgh that involves spontaneous gauge symmetry breaking (Higgs theorised that particles could acquire mass by "eating" a special force carrying particle now known as the Higgs Vector Boson. It has zero spin and a large mass). By describing the weak nuclear force in terms of gauge fields (there are three force fields: one each for the W^+ W^- and Z° force carriers) and then couple the gauge fields with the Higgs-field would break the gauge symmetry and give the W and Z particles a mass.

After their initial success, Weinberg and Salam proceeded to combine electro-magnetism and the weak nuclear force into a single gauge field theory in which there were now four force-fields. At this particular stage the W and Z particles were still massless. They then proceeded with spontaneous symmetry breaking by coupling the gauge fields with the Higgs field. The photon of the electromagnetic force is left untouched by this process and remains massless. Thus Weinberg and Salam proved that the weak nuclear force and electro-magnetism really are very different aspects of a single force – the electro-weak force. The evidence for the Weinberg – Salam theory came with the eventual discovery of the W and Z particles by researchers at Cern, Geneva in 1983. The masses of the W and Z° particles turned out to be 87 times heavier than the proton for the W's and 98 times heavier than the proton for the Z°.

The weak nuclear force plays an extremely important role in shaping the physical world. If it did not exist, the nuclear reactions in the stars could not proceed. If it did not exist or if its strength varied from its observed value, supernovae would not occur and none of the life-giving heavy elements could have permeated the physical world.

STRONG NUCLEAR FORCE

The strong nuclear force is known for "gluing" elementary "quark" particles into protons and neutrons and for holding the mutually repelling protons and the neutrons together as one unit – the atomic nucleus. However, the strong force involves baryons (e.g. protons and neutrons) as well as the short-lived mesons (e.g. pions and kaons) in combinations of three quarks or in quark-antiquark pairs respectively. The force-carrying particles which "commute" between the quarks, sticking them together in either pairs or trios, are appropriately called "gluons".

In the 1930's, there was still an unsolved mystery concerning the nucleus of an atom. How could it exist at all? Earlier experiments had clearly shown that the nucleus was made up of protons and neutrons and they all knew that protons carry positive charges and particles with similar charges repel one another. It dawned on physicists that there must be another, rather strong force in the nucleus that binds the protons together, counteracting the repulsion caused by their electric charge.

What could it be? Gravity was immediately ruled out as it was far too weak. The force was very short in range, effectively losing all its strength beyond a distance of about 10^{-13} cm from a proton or neutron. Both, protons and neutrons are subject to this pulling force but electrons are not. Because the influence of electromagnetic and gravitational forces is felt, albeit very slightly, throughout the physical world, the ultra-short range of this force was something new to the physicists at the time. It was this peculiar feature that led Hideki Yukana to a new way of thinking about the fundamental forces of nature. According to his theory, all forces are ultimately the result of special, virtual force-carrying particles "flitting from particle to particle" and back again. Because of the short range of the force he estimated the mass of these force-carrying particles to be about 270 times greater than that of an electron. He called them mesons, meaning "middle" (weights) in Greek.

It wasn't long after experimentalists began their search for mesons that the American physicist Carl David Anderson (who discovered the positron) found a particle that seemed to have the right mass. However, it turned out that what he found was the muon, an unstable particle belonging to the family of leptons. Finally, eleven years later in 1947, the British physicist Cecil Frank Powell discovered the elusive meson during experiments on cosmic rays. It was called Pi-meson and later changed to pion. Later they "discovered" that an entire family of mesons is responsible for making up the strong force.

Yukawa's revolutionary meson-based theory for the strong force was still relevant in the early 1960's when Robert Hofstadter and his colleagues at Stanford University in California fired electrons at protons by means of the two-mile long Stanford linear accelerator. After the impact, the trajectories of the electrons suggested that they were being deflected by hard little lumps inside the proton. Final results of these experiments proved that the theory proposed by Murray Gell-Mann and another American physicist, George Zweig in 1963 was sound. They stated that protons and neutrons were not elementary particles at all but were the result of combinations of other particles (Gell-Mann named them "Quarks") inside them. Later, experimenters at Cern in Geneva got further evidence that proved that the particles inside the protons and neutrons had fractional charges as predicted by the quark theory.

But why were the quarks so difficult to get hold of? A possible explanation was provided by the Stanford linear accelerator. Protons seemed to contain more than just quarks, in fact they seemed to have additional particles with no electric charge acting as some kind of "glue" within the proton, holding the quarks together. Obviously, some sort of force was needed to bind the quarks together. They named these force- carrying particles "Gluons".

Quantum chromodynamics (QCD), the theory of the action of gluons was introduced and built-up during the 1970s. The central tenet of QCD is: gluons prevent the quarks from escaping by gluing them by the so-called "colour force" which has the property to get stronger the further the quarks are from one another. This in itself is very odd as all the other forces of nature become weaker with distance. The inter quark force does the opposite. Not only does QCD describe the actions of quarks and gluons but because quarks make up protons and neutrons it became clear that the overall force between whole neutrons and protons must be merely a residue of the more powerful inter quark force. This obviously was the death-knell for Yukawa's meson-based theory for the strong nuclear force, having served its purpose for many years.

If there were no strong nuclear force, then nuclei could not exist and so again there would be no atoms nor molecules and no solid matter as we know, nor could stars generate heat and light from nuclear energy.

For my views on the origin of electromagnetism, gravity and the strong nuclear force, see "Movement and Forces".

STRINGS AND BRANES

STRING THEORY

According to leading physicists, the string idea was the most promising attempt toward a unified theory of the fundamental forces of nature, including gravity and capable of describing the physical world in a more complete and consistent way than previous theories. It superseded super-gravity which theorists finally thought was incurable. For a while the most powerful version of super-gravity with the greatest number of super-symmetry transformations was considered the leading contender for the ultimate unified theory of nature but with the rise of string theory in the mid 1980's, interest in super-gravity declined.

The string theory was revolutionary insofar as it re-interprets elementary particles as tiny **spinning and vibrating** bits of string-like objects with the strings vibrating in a different way for each different particle. The theory adds extra hidden spatial dimensions to our familiar four space-time dimensions, existing at every point in three-dimensional space. It also improves Einstein's theory of gravity to a quantum gravity theory without infinities in terms of new, more fundamental microscopic entities that resemble tiny vibrating and spinning elastic loops having the same properties as gravitons.

The mathematical construction of heterotic (hybrid) string theory of the 1980's can be pictured as follows: Step down to the unimaginable level of 10^{-35} metres and you are staring at the very fabric of space-time. The fabric's stitches are loop-like heterotic strings, **forever in motion,** constantly writhing around at great speed. It is an enlightening experience to see what we imagined to be myriads of point-like particles, force-carriers and those affected by them, are "in fact" heterotic superstrings, vibrating in their least excited state. Smeared around the strings are the characteristic "charges", be they electromagnetic, weak, strong or gravitational.

In the late 1980's, a number of technical problems concerning the complexity of the six extra dimensions convinced physicists to add membranes with two or more dimensions to existing one- dimensional strings. In principle these membranes are just multidimensional versions of string, their tension strictly related to string tension and the membrane's interactions purely geometrical in character. For practical purposes, physicists shortened the term membrane to "brane" and added a prefix to specify the number of dimensions it encompassed, e.g. a 0-brane is a point-like entity, a 1-brane is the established one-dimensional string, a 2-brane a two–dimensional membrane like a sheet and a 3-brane a boxlike entity. They are the current blooms of a geometrical garden, arisen from pointlike entities.

String theory saw the light of day in 1968 and the man indirectly responsible for its invention was the Italian physicist Gabriele Veneziano, working at Cern in Geneva.

In the late 1960's, physicists were completely bewildered by the great number and variety of subatomic particles that were produced in atom-smashing by giant particle accelerators. They wondered what the particles were for. The most problematic were the one's responding to the strong nuclear force, the hadrons, the family to which the protons and neutrons belonged. Most had very short lifetimes, in fact so short that they barely existed, mere "resonances" of their more stable relatives. Gabriele Veneziano, whilst taking the strange properties of these short-lived particles into account, developed and later proposed a formula that adequately expressed the features of hadrons. Soon after, physicists from across the globe tried to find out why the formula worked. In 1970, the physicists Yoichiro Nambu at the university of Chicago, Holger Nielsen at the Niels Bohr Institute in Copenhagen and Leonard Susskind at the Belfer College in Israel showed why the formula worked. The idea was intriguing to say the least. Gabriele Veneziano's formula could be deduced on the assumption that hadrons are tiny strings. The "resonances" were essentially different modes of vibrations of these strings.

Unfortunately, it soon showed that the string model for other particle families developed various abnormalities such as tachyons, a physically impossible particle that moves faster than light and for bosons, the theory made sense only in a world consisting of twenty six dimensions.

By the mid 1970's only a handful of physicists still devoted their time to the string theory. However, their diligence was rewarded when they found signs that string theory may be more than just a theory of nuclear particles. For example whilst trying to apply string theory to describe the strong nuclear force, calculations kept producing a particle that had no mass and two units of spin, something never produced by particle accelerators and thought of as just another abnormality. In 1974 the French theorist Joel Scherk and the American John Schwarz at the California institute of technology pointed out that just such a particle (the graviton) is demanded by the gravitational force as a force carrier. Schwarz's attention then turned to the quantum theory of gravity using a version of string theory developed by himself and Scherk in 1971 that needed a physical world of "only" ten dimensions and was free of tachions. These developments went largely unnoticed as most physicists/ theorists devoted their time to the quantum field theory. They missed out on a development just as revolutionary as Einstein's theory who reinterpreted three dimensional space as an elastic substance that can be stretched, compressed and distorted. In a similar manner, those tiny spinning and vibrating bits of string that look like geometrical curves with no width, can bend and turn in all possible ways just like an infinitely thin strand of rubber. They are perfectly elastic, so they can shrink to a point if necessary or be stretched out to an arbitrary length, beautifully complementing Einstein's vision. If a piece of string is stretched out in a straight line, the free ends pull together with a fixed force called the string tension. Specific quantized string vibrations and spins account for the many elementary particles that exist in nature whilst each new quantized state represents a set of physical properties like mass, charge and spin. What is baffling is the size of the strings representing photons, gravitons or electrons – less than a trillionth the diameter of a proton! Strings with two free ends could account for all known types of matter particles whilst strings with closed loops, just like tiny elastic bands vibrating and spinning in the right way, account for the force carriers of gravity – the gravitons. The string theory seems to automatically incorporate the elusive theory of quantum gravity and as an additional bonus it appears to produce sensible results, free of infinities.

In 1979, John Schwarz met Michael Green of Cambridge University at the nuclear research centre (CERN) in Geneva, where they both were intending to do some theoretical work over the summer holidays. Earlier on, Green had become captivated by string theory after studying Veneziano's original formula. After much discussion they decided to put their different careers on hold and start collaborating by following up an idea by Joel Scherk in 1976: combining string theory with super symmetry. Their first attempt was a failure but their persistence finally paid off. In 1981, after lots of hard work and lots of frustrations they celebrated their first success. A shortened version of superstring theory, as they called their hybrid theory, gave them an answer that was free of infinities and all the "nonsense" that goes with it. Although it was only a shortened version (that included gravity and all other forces), the theory seemed to keep its promise.

In 1982, they reduced the great number of possible super string theories to just a few with mathematics weeding out the flaws. In 1984, they reduced the remaining few to just one. It was free of infinities as well as other anomalies, something never seen before. During the year other physicists that up to this point in time were still working on the theory of super-gravity, started to take notice. The message from Green and Schwarz seemed to be: Replace your pointlike particles with ten dimensional, super-symmetric strings. Some big names in physics also began to take an interest in the super-string theory, notably Stephen Weinberg and the physicist and brilliant mathematician Edward Witten, a theorist at the institute for advanced study in Princeton, New Jersey. His involvement began shortly after Schwarz and Green demonstrated their anomaly free theory (it was Witten who showed a few years earlier, in 1981, that super-gravity, because of a technicality, could not be a "Theory of Everything").

The main thrust of new research into strings shifted now to Princeton in America where Witten worked. They confirmed that it was indeed possible for string theory to account for all four fundamental forces of nature. However, this could be improved if they combined the new theory with the old 26 – dimensional bosonic theory of the 1970's. David Gross, Jeffrey Harvey, Emil Martinec and Ryan Rohm, known as the Princeton String Quartet, married the new ten dimensional super string theory with the seemingly ludicrous 26-dimensional string theory. The combination, known as heterotic string theory (heterotic meaning hybrid) produced more ingredients to make a more realistic theory of elementary particle physics. In heterotic string theory ten dimensions are ordinary space-time dimensions of which six are compacted to invisibility and four that we now observe. The remaining sixteen are internal dimensions that enable heterotic strings (loops) to account for all the fundamental forces. It was unfortunate that the complex geometry of the six extra (compactified) dimensions finally still produced five different but mathematically consistent string theories. Nobody knew which of the five versions of geometry is the right one. As time went by, the full complexity of the six extra dimensions made string theorists realise that the five string models were incomplete insofar as they restricted themselves to one-dimensional strings. If they just expanded some strings to multi-dimensional entities they might be able to re-formulate the five models into one single theory. It was a matter of do or die.

MEMBRANES

Theorists were now forced to add more objects to the string theory which they called membranes or branes for short. They also changed the name of the one-dimensional string to 1-brane, called a two-dimensional sheet 2-brane, a three dimensional entity 3-brane and a point-like particle is referred to as 0-brane. As with particles and strings, for every brane there exists an anti-brane partner. All these alterations did not change the uniqueness of its mathematical structure because the tension of every type of brane is strictly related to the string tension and spinning still describes every possible type of particle.

In 1995, Witten showed that all five versions of string theory are actually mathematical reformulations of a single underlying theory – but there was more to come.

Several months later, the team of Witten and Petr Hořava at Princeton demonstrated a sixth version without any strings at all, based entirely on branes with two or more dimensions. This latest model, called M-theory (master theory), incorporates a space of ten dimensions instead of nine. It is a remarkable new geometrical picture that offers new insights into fundamental physics along the lines of Einstein's vision. Hořava and Witten's new physical world geometry consists of two closely spaced, flat, three dimensional (as in everyday life!), parallel branes resembling a double-glazed window. Each brane contains six additional curled-up (compactified) dimensions (important in determining the properties of matter particles and forces), making them nine (space) – dimensional. The gap between the two branes lies along the tenth dimension, the extra dimension that distinguishes the M-theory from the other five string theories. The branes are the boundaries of the extra dimension. Space only exists between the branes, not outside the gap. Our observable world with all its particles, forces and even light itself lies on one of the two branes separated by this tiny gap (approximately 10^{-30} centimetres across) from the other "hidden" brane world with its own set of (opposite!) particles, forces and light. The force of gravity exists and is felt throughout. Matter in the hidden brane world exerts a gravitational (pulling) force toward matter directly opposite in our brane-world and vice-versa. Gravitons are represented by tiny brane-bubbles floating forward and backward in the space between the two brane-worlds whilst some are stuck to the branes. All other particles (including force carrying particles) are also represented by brane-bubbles stuck to the brane-worlds.

It is great to know that Witten and Petr Hořava's M-theory and the following heterotic M-theory automatically incorporate the "tossed aside" super gravity because the theory of super gravity also incorporates Einstein's theory of relativity.

For cosmologists M-theory at first held many promises to improve the inflationary model as it seemed to offer ample opportunities for inflation to arise and subsequently, to end. However, the opportunities to fail also increased dramatically. There are myriads of ways to assemble the extra dimensions and combine them with branes and fields. A veritable landscape of possibilities with as many ways for them to fail.

A handful of physicists/cosmologists led by Paul J. Steinhardt, Professor of physics at Princeton University, New Jersey and Neil Turok, Professor of mathematical physics at Cambridge University followed a different direction. The source of their inspiration was the possibility of the two brane worlds moving back and forth, opening and closing the gap between them. The vital question was: what would happen if the two brane worlds collided? Would it produce an effect similar to the big bang?

STEINHARDT AND TUROK'S CYCLIC MODEL

If M-theory was right, a brane collision could be the equivalent to the big bang but without the brane worlds shrinking to zero size at the collision. The implications would be quite amazing, just imagine, time and space would have existed before the big bang!

In 1999, Steinhardt and Turok together with Ben Ovrut from the University of Pennsylvania laid the ground work to what later was to become, in the words of Stephen Hawking on the front cover of Steinhardt and Turok's book "The Endless Universe": "A challenging alternative to the accepted picture of the big bang and the future of the universe".

In the cyclic model, the big bang marks the moment when the two brane worlds collide at the end of a long period of slow approach. Hot, dense matter and radiation fills the physical world immediately after the bang. The cosmic temperature reaches about 10^{20} times that of the sun's core. However, it is not as hot as expected in the conventional big bang. Matter breaks down into elementary constituents, the likes of quarks, electrons and photons. The branes then rebound and structure begins to form in our brane world according to established scientific theories leading to the world we live in today, 13,8 billion years after the big bang. During the next trillion years, dark energy, the gravitational potential (self-repulsive) energy stored in the spring-like forces (that later draws the branes together), soon comes to dominate, pushing galaxies ever further apart until the physical world becomes uniform and pristine, devoid of the lumpy structures formed since the last big bang. Spring-like forces and gravity (its contribution ensures that the spring-like force never winds down) eventually bring the brane worlds together again. Because dark energy is unstable, it will decay near the end of the cycle into a form of extreme high pressure energy that causes the physical world to contract ultra-slowly, eventually leading to the next big bang. Unfortunately, a key ingredient which is the spring-like force that draws the two branes together at regular intervals, is assumed to exist. However, if we think of the two brane worlds as positive and negative components, the force of attraction could well be the spring like force. Perhaps one day a theory superior to M-theory may reveal the answer.

The emergence and subsequent birth of a viable scientific alternative to the inflationary, hot big bang theory was for me a joyous occasion because it incorporated a kind of opposite parallel world, something I anticipated long ago. It may not turn out to be the theory of the future as the discovery of gravitational waves from the BICEP2 telescope (located near the South Pole) would seem to rule out Steinhardt and Turok's cyclic model, but I sincerely hope that in the near future a variation of their theory might generate the required radiation. Ever since I gave some serious thought to the universally accepted theory of the hot big bang which is the abrupt appearance of our physical world out of nothing (and they meant it!), I found the theory from a philosophical view point totally unacceptable. Unfortunately, over the last seventy years no viable scientific theory of a physical world that expands and contracts at regular intervals supported my own philosophical view. The principal reason for this state of affairs was because the second law of thermo-dynamics did not allow it.

The law states that in any system isolated from outside influence, entropy (the measure of disorder in a system) always increases. In 1934, Richard Tolman, a professor at Caltech wrote the famous treatise "Relativity, Thermodynamics and Cosmology". In it he presented a compelling argument against a cyclic picture, based purely on entropy. Another blow against it was the discovery of the cosmic background radiation. It convinced scientists and the public at large, that the physical world had a definite beginning from "nothing". Following this, another blow came when Stephen Hawking and Roger Penrose in the 1960's and 70's showed that according to Einstein's theory of gravity, a shrinking universe (if it did contract) would end up in a state of infinite density (cosmic singularity). The irony is that according to GUT and inflation theory the physical world ought to have emerged from something like a singularity or – "nothing!" Now, if that would repeat itself at regular intervals . . . . . The final blow was astronomical "evidence" that the expansion of the physical world is accelerating and the concentration of matter is anyway too low for the world to contract and finally collapse. However, during all those years my hope scientists will find a viable theory for a cyclic physical world, never ceased. Circumstances change, new discoveries are made. As I have said, Steinhardt and Turok's cyclic physical world regrettably may not be the answer; I say regrettably, because their theory seems to have taken care of obstacles described above.

Critics and criticisms of the string and membrane picture of elementary particles and forces are plentiful, not only among physicists but also the public at large. Strings, membranes and M-theory owe their origin essentially <u>not</u> to observation but to abstract mathematics and because of the extremely small scales of strings and branes and the massive energies needed to test them, scientific evidence will be hard to come by.

My view is that science, in particular advanced cosmology and quantum physics will in the not too distant future become even more detached from so-called reality and human experience. Intuition tells me that theorists will not be able to express the underlying intricacies of systems and entities by ways of ordinary geometry and known mathematics. New means of systematic abstract thinking have to evolve to capture the inner riches of nature. I say this because, for example, nobody can at present with any kind of accuracy, describe the true structure and inner movement of an elementary particle. It is my view that if, after all this time of scientific manipulation, a particle is neither point nor grain-like nor anything else close to reality, there is no reason why it might not be any abstract form, however absurd it may seem as long as it fits sound available data and lies within the spectrum of possibilities. At least it is a step forward in the, hopefully, right direction. I am also convinced that sooner or later scientists will find ways to prove or disprove the validity of their theories by means other than conventional experiments. Whether it can still be called scientific, remains to be seen!

CONCLUSIONS

The essence of physical existence is movement, however, to our eyes some things move and others do not. Some cars are in motion, others are not. Rivers and streams are in flowing motion whilst mountains lie still. We should not generalise, we should not say "everything moves" or "there is movement everywhere" – or should we?

Our eyes see movements and stillness, activity and inertness – and it is good the way it is, however, it is all a façade. Behind it, beyond the reach of our eyes still mountains and stationary cars are grounded on planet earth and earth rotates around itself and around the sun. As passengers of our planet everything and anything is in motion, but this is not the end. If our eyes could zoom-in on the still lying mountain we could detect life, plenty of life moving about the inanimate, motionless rock. However, the seemingly motionless rock is another façade. Our eyes cannot see what rock is made of. If our eyes could zoom-in even more, much more onto and then into the barren rock we would discover something extraordinary – movements, movements everywhere. Molecules, the smallest portions of rock are in constant motion and, under higher magnification, inside, are atoms, also in motion. Subatomic particles make up the atom. Amid force-carrying photons moving back and forth, a swirling cloud of electrons is orbiting a nucleus consisting of protons and neutrons. They are also in motion because they are composed of vibrating, vortex-like spinning quarks amid swarms of shortlived, short range and strong-force-carrying gluons moving back and forth. The weak gravitational influence between particles, according to the physics hand-book, is mediated by shortlived, force carrying gravitons also in back and forward motion whilst spinning around in seemingly merry abandonment.

Yes, the still lying rock is just a façade and so are stationary cars, moving cars, houses, trees and everything else including ourselves – and good it is, the way it is. Behind the façade is movement, movement everywhere ....

The definition of movement is: "Change of position or place" but;

WHAT MOVES?

What really changes position or place?

In the world around us, in familiar territory, we profess to know what moves and what does not, but what about the microphysical world? What are so-called elementary particles made of?

The answer is: nobody knows for certain. The building blocks of our physical world are enigmas in the truest sense of the word. However, I trust that my theory of the elementary part of the microcosm via the realm of the abstract, will help unlock some of the mysteries associated with particles – or strings – or membranes!

Unlike strings and membranes which owe their origin to mathematics and advanced geometry, the concept of particle still retains some kind of reality, not too remote from human experience. One thing is certain, a subatomic particle (or string or membrane!) bears no resemblance to a grain of sand or particle of dust. These are physical objects. However, subatomic particles are not objects, not even "things" in the ordinary sense. Some physicists describe them as fuzzy pieces of "nothing", quanta or quantities of some entity or more abstract, as "tendencies to exist or happen" but most scientists feel that it is meaningless to even pose the question of what they are or what they consist of.

My attempt to describe the "structure" of an elementary particle of matter incorporates in my opinion the most possible and most likely concept of contained, intrinsic movement but is not based on physical principles or mathematics as I feel the <u>true</u> "structure" or inner workings of a particle, any subatomic particle, is, at this stage in time, beyond anybody's imagination or calculated geometry. Notwithstanding the fact that individual particle's effects are noticeable on instruments and, collectively myriads of them make up matter, radiation and forcefields (including you and me), my view is that elementary and force-carrying particles are still elements of the physical-material world but are not composed of anything we could describe at this stage in time as being physical-material (energy is a concept, its definition similar to power!). Particles are either tiny bits of movements or tiny, moving bits of movements of some underlying substance, extremely abstract, something that cannot as yet be defined in terms of physics.

My Theory of Existence will shed some light on what actually moves, therefore, to get a proper representation, we need to start at the beginning with a brief visit to the far-out "Primordial world" on existence level "Y. Here, **fundamental** existence depends on the movements of primordial entributes Pos, Neut and Neg, effectively causing "Primary motion power", the proto of universal movements and power. On this level Pos and Neg engage in an eternal dynamic, variable and inter-changing relationship of attracted opposites, optimally restrained by Neut, the most influential, third primordial entribute.

Closer to "home", advanced versions of the primordial entributes, namely U-minded Pos, Neut and Neg make up the Wholeness of the U-minded world on existence level "X". Their movements generate the power (U-minded motion power or Potentia) <u>to be and to do</u> anything conducive for optimal existence, <u>not in reality or fact but in possibility, probability and ···· certainty.</u>

Potentia partis are border movements and non-physical aspects of the nature of elementary particles. At this point, anything potential, probable or certain becomes factual. Idea-like movements become physical-abstract movements, flat – vortexlike spinning and vibrating bits of a specific substance in lasting or transient motion, making up "real" or virtual particles of forcefields; also bits of the same substance in physical-abstract, spherical – vortexlike spinning and vibrating motion in either forced nuclear states or forced states of motion around it, corresponding to elementary particles of matter.

Different movements and variations in movement account for the differences in the "vital statistics" of subatomic particles such as mass, spin and electric charge. But <u>what</u> moves at the end of our microcosm? What is this mysterious, almost mythical substance?

Supported by science (indirect evidence from quantum physics) I see absolutely no reason to suspect otherwise, it has to be residue from the primordial and U-minded worlds. For this reason I changed the names Pos, Neut and Neg collectively to **Substantia** and individually to **Posens, Neutens & Negens.**

They are the foundations of physical existence and necessary for the empowerment of forces, force-fields and the existence of matter and energy (Pos-ens; Neut-ens; Neg-ens; - ens, Latin, to be).

Substantia is primary substance and the collective **Medium of Movement,** a subjective-abstract means to an end.

The individual medium of movement (either Posens, Negens or Neutens) of any elementary particle of matter, radiation and force-field is explicitly revealed by the particle's either positive, negative or neutral electric charge which most possibly results from either clockwise, anticlockwise or combined spin respectively.

Particles of matter carry either positive, negative or neutral charge and most force-carrying particles, including the particles of electro-magnetic radiation (bosons), have neutral charge. Most force- carriers are "neutral agents" in the truest sense of the word, "authorised" (See U-mind) to "glue" (opposite <u>and</u> equally charged) particles of matter in optimal and meaningful ways. An elementary particle of matter with neutral charge is the neutrino, a ghostlike entity with very little rest mass (it moves close to the speed of light). Neutrinos are the most common particles in our physical system and it is possible that collectively they may influence cosmic gravity.

For every particle there is a counterpart which is its mirror image and opposite in major respects, for example the anti-particle of an electron with negative charge is the positron with positive charge. Some particles are their own anti-particle, most with neutral charge.

Polarity in physics is of greatest significance because ultimately all movements emanated from primordial polarity. Positive and negative electric charges and matter and anti-matter reflect in an obvious way the Pos – Neg foundation of our universe and together with neutral particles of matter, radiation and forcefields physically represent in a pre-eminent manner the main ingredients of the Principle of existence.

All matter can be decomposed into combinations of six quarks and six leptons. It is an interesting fact that all ordinary matter in our world is made from just the two lightest quarks (the "up" and "down") and the two lightest leptons (the electron and its neutrino). For example the main component of the atomic nucleus is the proton with a positive electric charge of 1-unit, made, according to the quark theory, from two up quarks with ⅔ of a unit positive charge each and one down quark with ⅓ of a unit negative charge (giving a net positive charge of 1-unit). The other component is the neutrally charged neutron, made from one up quark with ⅔ of a unit positive charge and two down quarks with ⅓ of a unit negative charge each (giving a net charge of zero). The electron around the atomic nucleus is an elementary particle with a negative charge of 1-unit.

Consequently, the effective, subjective-abstract medium of movement of, for example the down quark, is Negens; of the up quark Posens; of the electron again Negens (with different structure of contained movement to the down quark) and of the photon (the particle of radiation and carrier of the electromagnetic force) Neutens, incorporating both Posens and Negens in equal amounts.

PHYSICAL SUBSTANCE

Substance: Latin substantia, essence, property.

Substance in philosophy is understood as that out of which all things are composed. In ancient Greece, philosophy and physics both arose out of speculation on what such a substance is and how it changes into the things of every-day experience. Plato and Aristotle both regarded substance as a primitive, indefinable material shaped after the pattern of ideas.

Before we get stuck in a quagmire of conflicting ideas, I believe we have to distinguish between physical and metaphysical substance and the level presently under consideration is the physical domain. A priority therefore is to establish a borderline between the physical world and the world of the metaphysical-abstract. The subject of reality cannot be included because some branches of theoretical physics have overstepped or extended acceptable boundaries of reality. But where are the frontiers of physics and consequently the boundaries of our physical world?

It is no surprise that one of the most prominent physical boundaries is found in motion – the speed of light! No physical entity, information or signal involving the transfer of energy can travel faster than visible light or any other type of electromagnetic radiation. According to Einstein, the speed of light is the only universal (physical) constant. The value for the velocity of all types of electromagnetic radiation in a vacuum is close to 300,000 Kms per second. The speed in water, glass and other transparent media is less than the speed in air (which is slightly less than the speed in a vacuum).

The reason for the maximum velocity of electromagnetic radiation in a vacuum is the vacuum itself which is alive with activity. The emptiness of space is an illusion. The theory of relativity says that ordinary spacetime can bend, stretch or shrink, and gravity, in essence, is warped or curved space-time. At present space is in an accelerating expansion mode. But what are the contents of so-called empty space?

According to Heisenberg's uncertainty principle relating to the behaviour of energy, empty space ought to be full of virtual particles "popping in and out of existence!" These temporary particles cannot be seen even with the help of our most sophisticated instruments. However, they may leave physical traces as proof of their extremely brief existence. Just imagine, tiny ghostlike particles coming from "nowhere" and a trillionth of a second later, going to "nowhere!" And how much do we really know about dark matter and dark energy? Not much. These are some of the frontiers of physics indicating the present boundaries of our physical world. Beyond ordinary space-time, beyond the restrictions imposed by so-called empty space, our concepts of place and movements in time break down ....

Now then, in our quest to search and define physical substance, are we allowed to invent or include "strange" entities and concepts?

The answer is "yes" as long as it is reasonable and has the potential to be proven right. "Proof" can be established either by means of mathematics, observation, experiments, improved instruments, logical inference or preferably, by combinations of the above. However, it must be mentioned that boundaries between the physical and the metaphysical-abstract are getting less and less clear with the latest advances in the physical sciences. Just consider the string and membrane theories which are deeply rooted in concepts and structured by mathematics. Is the scientific fraternity not "pushing the envelope" a bit far? I would say no if there is the slightest possibility that the theory may bring humans closer to the truth, and this, in the end, is what it is all about ····

A few scientists, for example Alfred North Whitehead, Werner Heisenberg and Arthur Stanley Eddington treated substance as a subject of physics. From their standpoint the ultimate causes and the indestructible substance of the philosophers disappear and matter (!) is defined in physical terms, having an experimental meaning only. Matter becomes simply a set of events occurring in a gravitational field and these events are multiples of Max Planck's unit of Action (Planck's unit of Action, also known as Planck's Constant, is a basic element of quantum theory and represents the quantized nature of energy emission and absorption).

Not having detailed knowledge of their interpretation, all I care to say is that physical substance should not be limited to matter. In view of my theory that particles are "movements" or "moving movements", physical substance ought to transcend matter, radiation and forces. It has to be that which is fundamentally common to all manifestations of our physical world.

By natural consequence, matter, radiation and forces have all been quantized or, in more popular terms, reduced to elementary particles of matter and forcefields.

What are the properties of elementary particles? According to the physics handbook, most elementary particles of matter have rest mass (a form of energy), charge (a form of energy) and spin (a type of movement). Particles of forcefields have kinetic energy (a form of energy) and spin (a type of movement), as well as vibrations (another type of movement). In the end all the above properties can be reduced to energy and movement. But what do these particles really consist of? The answer is simple: Nothing tangible. The scientist's last hope is the rest mass of particles of matter which in my view is contained, concentrated movement. But even if the newly discovered (during experiments involving the large Hadron collider at CERN, Geneva) particle resembling the Higgs Boson will be positively identified as the particle that was responsible for giving every matter- particle mass, scientists will still not be able to explain the **essence** of rest mass.

This means that, in my view, all elementary particles have only two fundamental properties:

Movement and Energy.

Could movement be substance? Certainly not. Movement is activity and the word means change of position. To make sense, the particle ought to consist of something that moves, however, scientists do not know what this "something" is.

Why do I set "movement" on such a high level of importance?

Firstly, its universal manifestation in the macrocosm. Imagine a world without changes!

Secondly, in the subatomic realm, motion and movements are all-important. Subatomic particles are movements and movements in motion: waves, vibrations, vortex-like motion and other movements in unbelievable harmony.

Thirdly, the primary, inherent effects of my principle of existence are movements of opposites (held apart by an equally dynamic "Neut").

Could energy, in particular quantum energy, be substance? Certainty not. Energy is an abstract concept: "The capacity of a material body or of radiation to do work", a specific power to do, to create and to destroy. Energy/power must be caused by "some thing". It cannot be substance.

Yes, all "evidence" points to the fact that in the microcosm movement and energy are inseparably connected and because they are united, they have a common source. It is **Substantia, the media of movement, consisting of Posens, Neutens and Negens.**

Yes, the subjective-abstract, super-idealike, ordinary space-time conditioned media of microphysical movement-energy, **Substantia, is primary substance of our physical world.**

MOVEMENTS AND FORCES

The long overdue worldwide "Clean air Campaign" and the prospect of running out of crude oil by the middle of this century brought the spotlight onto carbonfree, renewable sources of energy. Solar, wind, electric battery and hydropower are the buzzwords of today. Windfarms with arrays of wind turbines are appearing around the globe anywhere there is reliable movement of air.

Yes, movement is power, but not only in the macrocosm, in the microcosm as well. Excited, freemoving electrons inside a copper wire provide us with the comfort of artificial light. Electromagnetic waves or, in terms of particles, photons, moving at the speed of light are utilised as signals for television, cell phones, etc. But even the free-moving electrons or the fast-moving photons themselves consist of movements – specific movements of Negens and Neutens respectively.

The physics handbook says that particles of matter are sources of force fields but does not say <u>why</u> forces and force fields exist or why a superforce initially existed.

In my view, elementary matterparticles are composed of specific movements of Substantia and it is these movements that "generate" the basic forces of nature.

Yes, the four forces of nature are direct expressions of the power of movement.

For example in an atom, electrons are orbiting the nucleus whilst simultaneously the orbiting electrons themselves are in constant motion. Their, in my view complex, possibly "anti-clockwise" vortex-like spin of Negens accounts for their negative electric charge.

The protons and neutrons of the nucleus consist of three quarks each. The two "up" quarks with possibly "clockwise" vortex-like spin (of Posens) in the direction of an inner centre and the one "down" quark with similar but anti-clockwise spin account for the net positive electric charge of the protons. The neutron's three quarks account for its net neutral charge. The force of attraction or in more technical terms, the electromagnetic forcefield between the protons and the orbiting electrons is due to their opposite electric charges. The force keeps the electrons (electron-cloud!) in optimal, stable orbit around the nucleus. Because the forcefield extends outside the electrons, other atoms exerting the same force joined to form molecules.

The strong nuclear force can be explained by the (either "clockwise" or "anti-clockwise") vortex-like standing spin of quarks (of either Posens or Negens) towards a hypothetical offset inner centre. Because protons and neutrons consist of three quarks each, the cumulative effect (combined pull) towards the hypothetical centres of protons and neutrons produced by the vortex-motion of each quark is enormous, enough to glue the quark trios firmly in place with ample inward force left over to stick the protons and neutrons together into a tight nucleus (the protons against their own repulsion caused by their positive electric charges!).

Gravity in my view is a residual force, a separate left-over from the strong nuclear force. The incredibly weak force of gravity emanating from the nucleus of an atom accumulates as more and more particles come together. Considering how weak the force is in the microcosm, it is ironic that in the macrocosm gravity is a major force. It is the cosmic glue that holds the physical world together.

Because of Heisenberg's uncertainty principle, it is impossible to describe particle form and contained movement but I am convinced that the complex and controlled vortex-like spin of Posens and Negens are ultimately the cause of our basic forces of nature. They are ingenious "inventions" of the U-mind, indispensible for creating the cycles of cosmic expansion and contraction, development and decay because, without the generation of forces, particles of matter would not exist.

However, there may be more, much more to the movements of Substantia than generating the four basic forces of nature, something inherently connected to the movements that "give birth" to the forces of nature: **Energy.**

ENERGY

The word originates from the Greek energeia-en, in; ergon, work.

Energy was introduced into physics as an abstract concept - the ability of a body to do work. For the physicist the concept of energy is of great appeal and considerable value, in the main because of the law of energy conservation. However, if you ask a physicist what energy really is, he or she may not commit him/herself to explain.

In physics, they define energy as **"the capacity of a body, system of bodies or radiation to do work".** In other words, energy is a specific kind of power in bodies or radiation - "the capacity to do work"! One cannot isolate "capacity for doing work" entirely from the word "power" because power means "ability to do" (anything) or "capacity for producing an effect". The word power is more colourful but unfortunately for us ordinary folks, in physics power is used to measure the rate at which work is being done or the rate at which energy is being expended.

The word energy and the meaning behind the word is cause for lots of confusion and misrepresentation. In many instances it has almost become part of reality. How often have we heard the following: "I haven't got enough energy to climb up those stairs" or, "the energy in a crystal enhances the power of mind". Some people say that energy is not material and at the next instance they state with great wisdom that all, including matter, is energy. The famous physicist Albert Einstein once described matter as "frozen energy". Light, often referred to as pure energy, can blind you and heat (another type of electromagnetic radiation of a different wavelength) can burn you whilst other types of radiation may not have any effect on you. One of the most elusive forms of energy is potential energy. Where is the stored (potential) energy (of position) in a weight placed on top of a shelf? Kinetic energy is energy associated with motion, for example a moving bullet has kinetic energy.

To get some clarity into our subject-matter, let us start at the very beginning.

In physics, work occurs when the application of force to a body causes the body to move. Such work is defined as the mathematical product of the force (F) x distance (l) through which the body was moved by the force. The product Fl represents **the work done on the body AND the energy imparted to it.**

For example: if I lift a weight of 10 kilograms onto a 2 metre high shelf, the work done would be (10 x 2) 20 kilogram-meters, regardless of how long it took. The exercise consumed some of my energy. The physicist says 20 kilogram-meters of energy has been expended. However the energy is not lost. The law of conservation of energy says that **energy is always conserved, never created nor destroyed but may be transferred from one form to another**

Where has the energy gone? It must still be there somewhere and indeed it is. 20 kilogram-meters of additional energy is now stored in the weight because of its higher location. The form my expended energy has taken is now called potential energy, it exists but it cannot be seen, however, it could be recovered by letting the weight crash down onto the floor. The stored energy would be released and transformed into other forms.

As mentioned before, the general meaning of power is the ability to do (anything) or the capacity for producing an effect, however in physics power measures the **rate at which work is being done** and **the rate at which energy is being expended.**

To come back to the previous example, the work done was 20 kilogram-meters and 20 kilogram-meters of energy has been expended. If I lifted the weight in two minutes and my brother lifted it in four minutes, the power exerted by me world be $\left(\frac{20}{2}\right)$ 10 kilogram-meters per minute and by my brother $\left(\frac{20}{4}\right)$ only 5 kilogram-meters per minute, in other words, if I work faster I exert (bring into active operation) more power and expend (employ/consume/spend) more energy.

It works well and it seems we are stuck with the word energy for a long time.

One of the most fascinating aspects of energy is its ability to transform from one form to another without loss as for example in motors and generators. What we intuitively think of as loss may in reality turn into gas, sound waves, heat and other forms of energy. Mechanical energy lost when work is done against friction appears as heat energy. In a pendulum the potential energy (the elusive energy of position) at each end of the swing is transformed to kinetic energy (energy of motion) at the middle and vice versa. Both of these forms are present at intermediate positions. The "energy of being" is the locked-up energy in the pendulum itself.

The energy locked-up in matter-particles is also "energy of being". Together with the kinetic energy of particles of electromagnetic radiation, electrons and neutrinos (the ghostly, most common particle of ordinary matter in the physical domain) and the energy of vacuum and force-carrying particles, they make up most of the known quantum-energy of our physical world. Little is known of dark energy, the majority of energy today according to leading cosmologists. Dark energy consists of a component that repels itself gravitationally and causes the expansion of the cosmos to accelerate, a kind of anti-gravity. Dark matter is another enigma. Believed to be the majority of the mass in our physical world, it consists of particles that gravitationally attract one another just like ordinary matter, however, do not scatter or absorb light. The locked-up energy In dark matter particles cannot be discounted.

QUANTUM ENERGY

There is certainly more to quantum energy (the energy of subatomic particles) than just "the capacity to do work" or even "the capacity to destroy a whole city in one sortie", as happened on August 6, 1945, when the American Air Force dropped an atomic bomb onto Hiroshima and practically obliterated the city.

Yes, at the subatomic level two entirely independent properties of matter, mass and energy, are uniquely united. The independence of mass (quantity of matter in any body, measured by its resistance to change of motion inertia) and energy (capacity of a material body or of radiation to do work) does not exist in the formalism of quantum theory and relativity. Particles of electro-magnetic radiation have no rest mass, however they have energy by virtue of their movement through space. The mass and therefore the energy of particles of matter (their rest mass) increases whilst in accelerated motion. The relationship between mass and energy was discovered by Albert Einstein when he was working on his special theory of relativity. It is expressed in his famous formula:

$$E = mc^2$$

His formula conveys the message that even the tiniest of particles has within it a tremendous amount of energy. It also says that because c^2 (the speed of light squared) is a constant, mass and energy are equivalent and interchangeable, mass is energy and energy is mass. In Einstein's words: "energy has mass and mass represents energy". In particle physics, mass is a form of energy;

mass – energy.

Depending on application, mass can be replaced by energy and energy by mass. Particle physicists regularly measure the mass of particles in energy units.

I am convinced that the restmass-energy of an elementary particle of matter (e.g. an electron or quark) **is inseparably connected to its contained, vortexlike-inward spinning motion. Matter particles in travelling motion have kinetic energy, meaning, energy possessed by a matter particle in virtue of its motion (mass-energy increase).**

The energy of an elementary particle with no (or very minimal) rest mass-energy (e.g. a photon or neutrino) **is inseparably connected to its travelling motion (kinetic energy).**

The mass-energy of matter particles can be vastly increased by means of accelerated motion, produced for example by powerful magnets in particle accelerators (imagine the brisk traffic of force carrying particles between the accelerating particles and the magnets!).

Yes, at the subatomic level mass-energy and kinetic energy are intimately and inseparably connected to movement. For example when an electron moves toward the nucleus of an atom with a certain velocity and it is slowed down by the electromagnetic field, it loses speed and the kinetic energy associated with it. However, this is immediately transformed into a photon of radiant energy, instantly travelling at the speed of light. The kinetic energy of the photon equals the kinetic energy lost by the electron and is proportional to the wave frequency of the radiation. The higher the initial velocity of the electron moving toward the nucleus, the higher its loss (and the kinetic energy associated with it), but equivalently the higher the kinetic energy of the created photon. Because a photon cannot go faster than the speed of light, the "gain in movement" is reflected in an increase in the frequency of electromagnetic waves. In other words, even though an increase in velocity is impossible, there is still an increase in "moving waves".

All evidence points to the fact that restmass-energy and kinetic energy in the subatomic environment could not exist without movement.

In my opinion, movements of Substantia, a still unknown quantity and (through circumstances) neglected phenomenon in the subatomic domain, is one of two fundamental movements of microphysical existence; the other indisputably is - particles in motion.

1　Movements of Substantia　　} Rest-mass – energy (matter particles)

2　Particles in motion　　　　} Kinetic energy (radiation and matter
　　(& movements of Substantia)　　particles in motion)
　　　　　　　　　　　　　　 } Force carrying particle energy
　　　　　　　　　　　　　　 } Vacuum energy

Movements/motion and Quantum energy are inseparably connected: Movement – Energy.

Energy is an abstract concept and Substantia is primary substance, however, the three individual parts of Substantia, namely Posens, Negens and Neutens, can be referred to as subjective-abstract entities, existing in the physical domain without a trace of objective reality.

The following question may arise: "which of the two physical constituents came first, movement or energy?"

The question is similar and as senseless as the following question: "what came first, the chicken or the egg?".

No, if there ever was a beginning to our physical-cyclic system, movement and energy in the microcosm would have unfolded together from a common source (U-minded motion-power, known as Potentia) many, many cycles of physical existence ago. Although I have reason to believe that movement plays a primary role in the universe*, primary microphysical movements in ordinary space-time have evolved in conjunction with energy.

During each consecutive big cosmic crunch, specific movements of Posens, Neutens and Negens (remember, in my scheme, matter, el. charges and the forces of nature originate from specific movements of Posens, Neutens and Negens) compress into kinds of proto-movements, only to evolve again after the immediate big bang. How ever the big crunch may occur, violent or "sedate" (in the Steinhardt-Turok cyclic model, the collisions between the two branes

---

*　The universe consists of the primordial, U-minded and physical worlds.

occur at modest speeds, well below the speed of light)*, the inherent power of the proto-movements of Posens, Negens and Neutens (primal energy) ought to survive the hottest and most dense conditions. Failing this, the big crunch may end in a transubstantiation (Substantia into U-minded substance - Energy into Potentia) for an instant and, vice versa, trigger a quantum fluctuation in the vacuum of empty space followed by the next big bang . . . .

---

*   Also the reason why it cannot generate gravitational waves. With the recent discovery of gravitational radiation, the Steinhardt-Turok theory seems to have become obsolete (at least for now!).

WHY MOVEMENTS?

The following is a brief summary of the metaphysical origin of movements. The abstract concept leading up to it is introduced in Chapter 4, "The Principle of Existence".

Our entire physical world is movement and energy. However, notwithstanding the fact that movements of Substantia (primary physical movements) and quantum energy are inseparably connected, primary physical movements still seem to play a leading role. Why? The answer is found in what I call **Primordial*** **Agitation****, the primary, inherent effect of the principle of existence.

Primordial agitation is a combination of subjective-abstract primordial disturbance/turmoil/ excitement; in farfetched human terms one could compare it to stirred emotions or agitation of mind and, as we all know well, stirred emotions can be extremely powerful; they call for action! Similarly with primordial agitation. On the extreme upper level of our universe it evokes and exerts incredible movements and power (primary Pos – Neut - Neg motion-power) and as such it is a kind of precursor to all movements and energy in our physical world. Primordial agitation and primary non-physical Pos – Neut - Neg motion-power "occurs" in the primordial world on existence level "Y"****.

The inherent effects of the principle of existence applied to our physical world via Substantia, and the four fundamental forces of physical nature are the cause of all of physical nature's activity (movements). However, physical world movements cannot be compared with the subtle raw, subjective-abstract, primary, non-physical motion-power on existence level "Y". "Our" specific movements of Posens Neutens and Negens are modelled (not designed) by the U-mind into spinning, vibrating and free moving (tiny) bits of energy (particles).

---

*   Primordial means first existent. First here does not mean first in time, but of the first order, primary rather than secondary.

**   Latin: agitare, frequentative of agere, to put in motion.

***   Because the primordial and U-minded worlds are firmly anchored in a multi-layered, eternal present (as seen from our frame of reference), past or future as we know does not exist in the realm of these worlds.

Particles of matter with "conspicuous" vortex-like inward spin generate the four fundamental forces of physical nature and these forces, restrained and therefore protected by the laws of conservation, are responsible for the remaining activity/movements in our physical world. But primarily and fundamentally it is primordial agitation and primary, non-physical Pos – Neut - Neg motion-power that are ultimately responsible for all movements in the universe.

WHY ORDER, HARMONY AND PERMANENCY?

How can we explain the wonders of existing order, harmony and permanency in our ever changing world, its uniformity, coherence and beauty in structure? Why isn't the world engulfed in arbitrary and aimless random activity with particles moving about criss-crossing and colliding, or millions of stars colliding and exploding among heaps of galaxies in turmoil? Instead we observe a beautifully balanced cosmos filled with outward moving clusters of galaxies and galaxies filled with clusters of stars, nebulas and planets all moving in an orderly manner for millions of years. The same overall balance, order and harmony can be observed in the microcosm where myriads of particles act as building blocks of our physical world and above all, how can we explain the overall balance in the incredible diversity of living nature? How can such a multitude of different lifeforms exist in order and harmony, providing for and feeding of each other during their allocated time of life?

Logically, it doesn't have to be this way . . . .

Yes, balance is the magic word, not static but diverse and dynamic acts of balance, sometimes even but mostly varied with some of them resembling tugs of war. The entire cosmos and many of its intricate structures are products of what looks like tugs of war. These dynamic balancing acts are important in the make-up of our physical world. A premature or total win of either side could mean failure of the system. Let us glance at two of the most impressive competitions, one predominantly one sided and the other carried out on "the edge of a knife".

The cosmos is the playground for the most gigantic contest between the two most powerful opponents known to humankind. Here, the overall dynamics of our entire cosmic world depends on the tug of war between an expansionary force exerted by the dark energy, and the opposing gravitational forces exerted by galactic clusters, galaxies and dark matter with dark energy presently having the advantage. However, this superiority will inevitably end in the distant future when inward pulling forces regain strength, contracting matter and other types of energy. A gigantic crunch will herald the end of our cycle only to give impetus to the next big bang in order to restart another cycle of physical existence.

This is the most impressive example of a variable contest between two major opponents and typical for movements of a cyclic nature.

Also in the cosmos but on a much smaller scale an entirely different, hair-raising balancing act is performed between the opposing forces of gravity and electromagnetism inside a star. Gravity tries to crush the star but electromagnetic forces successfully act against the crushing force of gravity. A change in the strength of either force by only one part in 10^{40} parts would spell disaster for a star the size of our sun!

Equilibrium is a state of even balance, a state in which opposing forces, tendencies or influences neutralise each other. In the physical sciences it is a local static condition of minimum energy and thus maximum stability, for example static electricity is electricity at rest. It is present in most bodies by way of positively charged protons and negatively charged electrons in equal numbers. This neutralisation of opposite charges ensures stability of matter and permanence of physical existence.

Closer to home, on our planet, we witness less essential but more noticeable acts of balance. For example the "balance of nature" relating to animate and vegetative existence is a state of equilibrium in the incredible diversity of living nature, a state in which generally no particular type, group or family of fauna and flora fully dominates to the exclusion of others. Living nature does readily and in our eyes often cruelly dispose of or reduce in numbers forms of life that upset its diversity and natural balance, cannot adapt to certain specific conditions, have completed their natural cycle of life or existence or are at the wrong place at the wrong time. Most activities of living nature on our planet have settled down to reasonably stable states with the possible exception of one: Human activities! We ought not to forget that as a destructive force, we are, in the greater scheme of things, expendable!

A balancing act in nature, especially living nature, is an activity that requires the achievements of a balance not only between opposites but also between more than two, often innumerable parts or requirements and they do not always have to be equal in quantity or strength but have to be **in appropriate proportions**.

Development/evolution created complexity. It started shortly after the big bang at the beginning of cosmic expansion when quarks condensed into protons and neutrons and later combined with electrons to form atoms. From there onward, development could not be stopped. Most entities, bodies or systems that emerged, developed appropriate proportions of elements conducive for existence and further development. The complexity of advanced life forms demanded the achievement of a delicate balance between the combined operations of different systems and the incredibly high numbers of constituents.

We are aware that the instructions for building this great world of ours are contained in the laws of nature, specifically physics and the rules of mathematics and we know that some of these laws are extraordinarily fine-tuned, but what is the underlying principle to which a supercomputing U-mind laid down these laws and rules? What is the principle on which the order, harmony, permanency, uniformity, coherence and beauty of our physical world is based?

Fundamentally, existence depends on the dynamic, non-physical quality of attracted opposites Pos and Neg, optimally restrained by Neut.

Neut is short for neuter (Latin: neuter; ne, not, uter either), meaning neither. In my theory "Principle of Existence", Neut is one of three primordial entributes separating opposites Pos and Neg on existence level "Y".

In the realm of fundamental physical existence (elementary particles of matter, force-fields and anti-matter), Neut's physical manifestation is Neutens, effecting the state of equilibrium (even balance), a state in which opposites (positive and negative charged particles) have neutralised each other or are naturally neutralised, for example the result of matter-anti-matter particle collisions are photons which are electrically neutral. Most particles of forcefields are electrically neutral. Fully neutralised particles have always Neutens as their media of movement.

Neut's power to restrain is deeprooted, however, its source does not exist in the realm of Being. All that exists is a "distinct shadow of a distant idea", a kind of all-powerful residue from "the split of the Absolute" ("the uncaused self, independent of relation to other things").

I formulated my Principle of Existence on the premise that the Absolute is split into two different parts, opposites Pos and Neg with Neut confined in between (there is no "Before" or "Beyond" the split). The split causes (Primary cause!) primordial agitation (Primary effect!), primary motion power and a primordial mind, set on raw, balanced movements, and as a consequence causing raw balanced existence; all this on Existence Level "Y" ("lower down" on Existence Level "X", these "processes" result in U-minded motion-power known as Potentia and further "down" movement-energy on our familiar levels of existence "A", "B" and "C").

If primordial agitation and primary motion-power is caused by the split of the Absolute (into Pos, Neut and Neg), it is self-evident that **the Absolute cannot exist. However, as an all-powerful remnant of the primordial split, Neut plays centre role between Pos & Neg**

Nevertheless, a deep-seated "yearning" for self-existence and freedom from everlasting motion persists within Neut but remains unfulfilled because of its ultimate "position" between the two opposites. With Pos and Neg trying to unite in dynamic surges but prevented from doing so by Neut and the primordial mind being focused on balanced movements and optimal existence, the stage is set for a scenario of everlasting, raw, but generally balanced movements (primary motion-power).

See Figure 3.

Permanently forced to act as dynamic partition, Neut prevents Pos and Neg from fully uniting and due to its unifying disposition, it also prevents them from unintended movements away from each other's force of attraction (into oblivion!).

EXISTENCE LEVEL "Y"

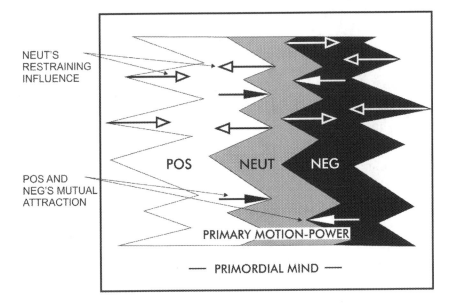

THE DYNAMICS OF BALANCED, PRIMARY MOTION-POWER

FIGURE 3.

Vice versa, dynamic Pos and Neg prevent Neut from inert stagnation, the death knell of existence.

The three primordial entributes and a primordial mind provide the foundation for optimal existence and continuity thereof, and their interactions constitute the principle for a balanced, harmonious, coherent and permanently moving physical world on considerably "lower" levels of existence.

It is worth remembering that in the physical world the movements of Posens, Neutens and Negens are "harnessed" and "re-modelled" representative movements of the ever moving primordial entributes Pos, Neut and Neg, re-directed to rules and laws disposed by the U-mind on Existence Level "X".

Yes, myriads of subatomic particles, great physical structures, impressive natural processes and above all, intriguing interactions between movement-energy and the forces of nature bear testimony to the success of this grand scheme.

"Down to earth" manifestations of the primordial opposites Pos and Neg and their movements are plentiful. They are found in every facet of human existence. The one closest to us, most impressive and in many instances almost "ruling our lives" are the everchanging highs and lows of our emotions (the movements of our feelings). In some rare cases normal mood changes can develop to extremes. The state of extreme feelings of euphoria followed by deep and destructive depression is called manic-depressive psychosis. Another important manifestation of Pos and Neg are the words of affirmation and negation "yes" and "no". Other opposites that play important roles in our lives are male-female, rich and poor, good and bad, love and hate, introvert-extrovert, black and white and many more.

Although opposites are the driving force for all our systems, starkly represented and indispensable in all spheres and levels of existence, stable matter, particles of forcefields and most forms of life need or are most comfortable in moderate or optimal situations or conditions between opposite extremes. The main reason why the physical world is in a state of balance, harmony, uniformity, coherence and parts of it in different optimum grades of permanency is fundamentally due to the calming, moderating influence of Neut and the U-mind's disposal of the ingenious laws and rules of nature on existence level "X". These allow physical and biological development, leading to increased choices and greater complexity whilst, in principle only, still submitting to the same subtle, raw, overall balanced "set-up" on Existence Level "Y".

4

PRINCIPLE OF EXISTENCE

THE ABSOLUTE (LEVEL "Z")

**The uncaused self, independent of relation to other things.
The Absolute cannot exist In the realm of being.**

In being, everything depends on something else for its existence. This rule applies up to and including the primordial world, Existence Level "Y", the "highest" level of existence. Even the primordial world consists of three primordial entributes (Pos, Neut and Neg), permeated by a primordial mind. A beyond does not exist. Existence is timeless. However, to satisfy the enquiring, timebound human mind, I devised a "Timeless Beginning" to existence: "The split of the Absolute" (into Pos and Neg with Neut taking a central role). As there is also no past and no future as we know on Existence Levels "X" and "Y", it is futile here even to speculate about the dimension we call "time".

In the realm of existence, the Absolute is and will remain a human idea, however, to commemorate the important role it played (and still does!) in the human mind, I located it to Level "Z" (not Existence Level "Z"). The following is an example of an out-dated, traditional view of "The Absolute":

In the order of existence (!) the absolute is infinite being, not restricted by limitation to a particular kind of entity or being as for example a grain of sand or animal, both of which are limited because there are other entities or beings of the same kind. In this order, the absolute possesses all the perfections of existence and is the source of being in things that exist in a particular way (how?), for example, as a grain of sand or animal.

The term absolute is used in other ways, all of which depend on its use in terms of being.

Common uses in the sciences are "absolute motion", "absolute alcohol", "absolute pitch" (in music the pitch of a note as determined by the number of vibrations per sec) and "absolute temperature" (absolute zero temperature). In terms of common thought we find it in the expression "absolute fact" (absolutely!).

PRINCIPLE OF EXISTENCE

EXISTENCE: latin, existere, exsistere: to stand forth.

**Minimal Fundamental Existence requires
a dynamic relationship of opposites**

No single fundamental "anything" could exist on its own.

**A primordial Entribute* can only exist in a
dynamic primordial relationship of opposites**

---

*   Entribute is a unification of "Entity" (a being) and "attribute" (quality, property
or characteristics). The primordial opposites Pos and Neg, are neither entities nor
attributes (nor just "anything").

EXISTENCE LEVEL 'Y'

THE PRINCIPLE (See Figure 4).

The Absolute is split into primordial entributes Pos, Neut and Neg, moving forever.

Neg is short for negative, Pos for positive and Neut for the latin word neuter, meaning neither.

To avoid any connotation to anything that may revoke universality (as for example Yin and Yang with their predominantly female-male connotation), I used the words Pos and Neg (symbolising primordial opposites).

In a strict sense, negative (underlying Neg) is the opposite to affirmative, however, generally accepted as that which is opposite, contrary to, or neutralising that which is regarded as positive (underlying Pos).

For example positive electric charge is opposite to negative electric charge and in mathematics positive is conventionally regarded as greater than zero and negative as less than zero with the positive sign being the plus sign (+) and the negative the minus sign (-).

The view that the negative may signify something bad or less than good originates in the human mind and is, from a human point of view only, in many instances fully justified. However, in the greater scheme of things exists an implicit unity of opposites:

One opposite cannot exist without the other. They are united in a conjugate relationship, separated by Neut.

Neut, symbolising neutrality and even balance (equilibrium), means neither Pos nor Neg, but it does not mean zero or nothing as it is a primordial entribute in its own right.

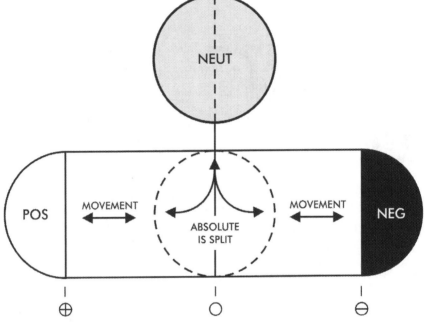

EXISTENCE LEVEL "Y"

THE PRINCIPLE OF EXISTENCE

FIGURE 4

"To be" and "not to be" arise mutually. LAO-TZU, 479 B.C.

This aphorism by Lao-Tzu "says it all", however, we must remember that in terms of universal being, nothingness or non-existence cannot exist. From an ontological point of view and for all practical purposes, it is the very negation of existence. Non-existence may not exist, however "things" either exist or do not exist. The cipher zero in mathematics stands for no-thing or nothing.

Although nothingness/non-existence in terms of universal being cannot be said to exist, it still looms as "shadowy background" in a conjugate relationship with existence.

THE PRINCIPLE OF EXISTENCE
AND ITS INHERENT EFFECTS

The "timeless split" of the Absolute and "consequential" existence of Pos, Neut and Neg

"causes" (primary Cause)

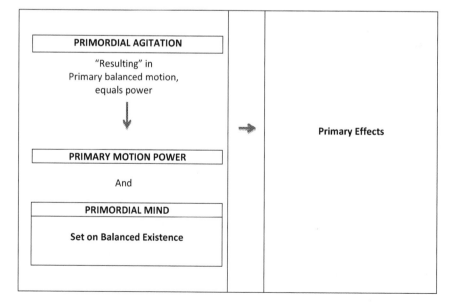

Motion in our physical world means "the act, state or manner of changing place or position", however, motion on Existence Level "Y" (primary motion!)

is not familiar space-time dependent motion. It is subjective-abstract, idealike, consisting of raw but generally balanced movements of primordial Pos, Neut and Neg in an, from our point of view, everlasting present.

Primary motion and power ("the capacity for producing effects") are inseparably connected.

THE WORLD OF FUNDAMENTAL TRUTH AND REALM OF PRIMARY CAUSE AND EFFECTS SHALL BE KNOWN AS THE:

PRIMORDIAL WORLD

(EXISTENCE LEVEL "Y")

THE TRIAD

Latin, trias; Greek, trias, triados-treis, three.

It means a group or union of three.

OMNE TRIUM PERFECTUM (FIGURE 5)

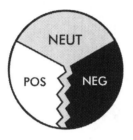

THE TRIAD

The Triad symbolises the three primordial entributes, the primary principle and essence (inner distinctive nature) of all being.

It synthetises a and b,:

a) The principle of existence and primary cause: The split of the Absolute into two different parts, opposites Pos and Neg, with Neut in between.

b) Primary effects:
    Primordial agitation "resulting" in balanced interactions between Pos, Neut and Neg that generate **primary Motion-Power and a primordial Mind, set on balanced existence.**

YIN AND YANG

"Opposites" play an all-important part in human life as some of them are most expressive since time immemorial. They are profoundly separated in the western world (definitely more so in in the past than at present) with traditional life revolving around good and evil, God and the devil, darkness and light, heaven and damnation, male and female, rain and sunshine etc. If someone would have told a God-fearing person living in western Europe four hundred years ago that an implicit unity exists between God and the devil or good and evil, he or she would most certainly be accused of blasphemy.

Not so in the east. Attention was drawn to this implicit unity of opposites as long ago as 2500 years by two philosophers: Heraclitus, born in Ephesus, an ancient Ionian city in Western Asia Minor (now Turkey), and the Chinese founder of Taoism, Lao-Tzu, born about 604 B.C., 54 years before the birth of Confucius. The following is a small selection of aphorisms written by Heraclitus that reveals his great insight into the hidden unity of opposites:

> "Opposition brings concord. Out of discord comes the fairest harmony".

> "It is by disease that health is pleasant; by evil that good is pleasant; by hunger satiety; by weariness, rest".

> "In the circle the beginning and the end are common".

> "To be in agreement is to differ; the concordant is the discordant. From out of all the many particulars comes oneness and out of oneness come all the many particulars."

> "The way up and the way down are one and the same".

> Homer was wrong in saying "would that strife might perish from amongst Gods and men." For if that were to occur, then all things would cease to exist.

The views of Heraclitus made no impact on the future of our Western culture. The last two thousand years of our culture was built mainly on the false view that the ideal present or "afterlife" is a life of pleasure without pain, light without darkness and good without evil. The realisation that life is not a one way street, nor ideal or fair, that good people may suffer and bad be rewarded does not perturb us as all we have to do is create an afterlife where justice prevails!.

In contrast to western culture, early Chinese civilisation was (and in the main still is) based on the principle of polar opposites. Lao-Tzu reminded us with the following words:

> "When everyone recognises beauty as beautiful, there is already ugliness".
>
> "When everyone recognizes goodness as good,
>
> there is already evil".
>
> "To be and not to be arise mutually;
>
> Difficult and easy are mutually realized;
>
> Long and short are mutually contrasted;
>
> High and low are mutually posited and before and after are in mutual sequence".

The foundations of Chinese culture, the ancient teachings and traditions and subsequent revisions and additions are compiled in the "I Ching" or "Book of Changes". Here we come across the archetypal poles of nature in graphic designs of hexagrams and trigrams consisting of broken and unbroken lines. The broken lines represent "Yin", the symbol of femininity, softness, yieldingness and also darkness and negativity, and the unbroken lines represent "Yang", the symbol of masculinity, hardness, strength as well as light and positiveness.

Although most of the characteristics associated with Yin and Yang have natural connotations, the "Supreme Ultimate" (t'ai chi, "that which has no pole but is the supreme pole" or "the implicit unity of the opposites"), possesses a mythical quality. According to ancient Chinese teachings, it is the "Supreme Ultimate" that created Yin and Yang. Its movement (!!) first produced the Yang and when resting, it produced the Yin. After the event, the two opposites proceeded with the eternal interplay and wavelike (!) movements that characterises everything in this universe. This is called "the way" (Tao). The movements never accentuate the extreme negative nor the extreme positive. There is no fundamental bad or fundamental good as isolated qualities as each one carries part of the other's within. Goodness and harmony is only found by the avoidance of extremes and by maintaining a healthy, dynamic balance. The dynamics in turn produces "the renewal of everything" which is called "the changes".

The familiar symbol of Yin and Yang is a circle, the "t'ai chi", and inside the circle are the two tadpole-like designs, one black and one white, each with one "eye" of the opposite colour. The design signifies rotation, movement without beginning or end (see figure 6).

YIN AND YANG

FIGURE 6.

One can imagine Yin and Yang in action when dream-like you stare into the sky watching the endlessly changing clouds revealing clear blue sky here and there, and even in the midst of pouring rain or in the cold darkness of the night, you know that there is, not too far away, sunshine and warmth.

Condensed to a few words, the above describes one of the wisest and most profound ancient philosophies ever conceived. No traditional western philosophy of existence nor traditional main- stream religion matches the depth of wisdom and rationality of its Chinese counterpart. The idea that explicit opposites have an implicit unity was (and to a great extent still is) inconceivable to mainstream western culture.

Unfortunately, Taoism evolved and its purity of thought became tarnished. From the 3rd to the 7th century, it took over many Buddhist features and beliefs, created a liturgy, established monasteries and developed an enormous canon of sacred writings. It accepted the doctrines of re-birth and karma and the belief in multiple heavens. More and more it concentrated on such objectives as seeking the elixir of immortality and finally it wasn't much more than a complex of superstition.

U-MIND (UNIVERSAL MIND)

The U-Mind is a derivation of the primordial mind. In my preamble to "Human Mind", I described the individual human mind as a "tiny", abstract-existent entity, a space-time bound, unsophisticated replica of the U-Mind, a "tool" enabling humans to survive, develop, create and, on a higher level of thinking, to establish and develop a conscious connection to, and understanding of – the U-Mind.

An indirect basic connection to the U-Mind exists in the microcosm in all subatomic particles (the potentia aspect of a particle's nature). Evidence of this connection is found in organic nature: an "inner desire" for fulfilment expressed in the "will" to exist, to survive, to live the cycle of life as best as circumstances allow, the desire to procreate and reproduce, to sprout, bloom and to seed. In animals, instinct is an involuntary "prompting to action", the natural impulse by which animals are guided, apparently independent of reason or experience. There is no doubt that during the positive phase (cosmic expansion) of each cycle of physical existence, organic nature is disposed toward development and growth **as if programmed to do so.**

However, during the negative phase of each cycle, organic nature will gradually cease to exist as cosmic contraction, retrogression and finally destruction sets in. Contemplating this inevitable future state, some people may ask the following questions: Why do we have to experience a negative phase? Where is the U-mind in times of cosmic destruction?

These questions are again typical of predominantly western thinking. Western cultures celebrate the illusion of neverending expansion, growth and development in every facet of existence.

> **However, the U-Mind has its own agenda. It is primarily set to preserve and possibly improve the greater scheme (consisting of the minded and physical worlds) and for physical existence to prevail in terms of space and flow of time, the world <u>has</u> to pass through a negative phase. Lesser things, however good in our eyes, will have to perish so that particles and forces can "re-charge" and re-organise themselves in order to rise and unfold again and again ….**

Another important fact has to be emphasised. It relates to the individual biological being:

Whilst the physical world passes through the positive phase each cycle, the U-Mind is only interested in the overall performance. It is not set to favour an individual human, animal or plant if circumstances are against it, however useful, beautiful and generally innocent and good from our point of view. However, nature provided powerful means to survive and develop: superb chemical structures, diverse adaptable bodies of incredible shapes and sizes, some equipped with super-efficient nervous systems and instincts, others with brains ranging in quality from primitive to super-complex and minds, mostly basic but others with great potential for further development. The potential power of the human brain and mind is beyond anyone's imagination and, casting scepticism aside, ought to guide us into an interesting and challenging future.

If you are having doubts concerning the existence of a U-Mind, consider the following:

> **The essence of physical existence is movement and, with "our eyes wide open", we discover movements, movements everywhere, most of them structured to a plethora of harmony, order and Direction.***

> **In the order and harmony of nature and the clear direction it takes, we discover Mindfulness and because order, harmony and direction are realised by strict adherence to super-constructive laws and rules, I conclude that there must exist a kind of "super-inventive" natural disposition, inclination or tendency which I call**

> **U-Mind, short for "Universal Mind".**

The negative, destructive phase of our cycle of existence is complementary and necessary, required for the purpose of continuity of existence. During the negative phase, the canvas of physical existence is swept clean in order to accommodate another master-piece. Each cycle, the painting is re-done, but the canvas stays, possibly forever. For this reason we have to conclude that:

---

*   Meaningful Creation

The U-Mind is a gigantic, super-fantastic ONE TRACK MIND, its "only" aim and purpose:

OPTIMAL EXISTENCE AND CONTINUITY THEREOF . . . .

and the purpose of the universe is:

-- TO BE --

Yes, scientists may soon be able to explain how all the physical structures in our world have come to exist automatically as a result of natural processes, but they will not be able to explain how the laws of nature, in particular the laws of physics and the fundamental constants, came to exist. This can only be explained by reference to the existence of a **U-Mind, absorbed on levels beyond ordinary space-time.**

A minority of scientists believe that the physical world "must have invented itself" to the level of its present functionalism over many cycles in an evolution-like process, possibly from another, inferior method of physical existence. I fully endorse this possibility, however, I do not agree with "invented itself" if it is meant without some kind of guidance from beyond ordinary space-time. Does the present order and harmony prevailing, for example in a well-run major city prove that it "invented itself" to the level of its present functionalism (over many hundreds of years) in an evolution like process? It may seem so. It may have progressed from small beginnings, but did the building plans and the laws and rules for efficient control of the city "invent themselves?" No.

Wherever it may be and in whatever scale of time, deeply hidden beyond all movements is a Mastermind.

The U-Mind is a derivation of the primordial mind. This "original" and "rudimentary" mind "occupies" the primordial world on existence level "Y".

In the same universe and, according to our scale of time, still in the realm of eternal present, is another world where our **U-Mind,** set on "optimal existence and continuity thereof", is in full and direct (top layer) and indirect (middle and bottom layers) control.

This is the Wholeness of the U-minded world, "taking up" Existence Level "X" "situated between" the primordial and the physical worlds. In this domain, power is vested in U-minded motion (U-minded motion-power), also known as Potentia, the complementary, subjective counterpart to our physical world's Movement-energy. Here, divergements of the primordial entributes (of the primordial world!) changed to U-minded Pos, Neut and Neg (only for divergements of U-minded Pos, Neut and Neg to change again in our ordinary space-time physical world to Posens, Neutens and Negens). From the Wholeness of the U-minded world (top layer), the U-Mind "disposes" the laws of nature including the laws of physics, its fundamental constants, the rules of mathematics and indirect, the four forces of nature (the implementation of the forces by means of specific movements of Substantia).

The U-Mind exerts an indirect controlling influence over the physical world via Potentia-partis, the non-physical, Potentia aspect of every subatomic particle's nature.

To avoid any misunderstanding it must be emphasised that the U-mind is not a super-natural intelligence or super-being who deliberately designed and created the physical world and everything in it.

"Derived" from the primordial mind, the U-Mind is an inherent property of the nature of Wholeness, an all-powerful **"NATURAL DISPOSITION"**, fully committed to optimal existence and continuity thereof. . . .

THE HUMAN MIND, THE U-MIND AND THE PURPOSE OF HUMAN EXISTENCE

Humans and possibly other intelligent forms of life in different locations of our physical world play a major role in the greater scheme. Far from being irrelevant and lost among the stars and dust of our cosmos, they are the only space-time dependent living creatures that bring the universe into Being, purely on the level of intellect. Yes, the universe is **realised** by a tiny, as yet crude and unsophisticated replica of the gigantic U-mind - the Human mind. Objects, matter and forms have no independent reality of their own. Homo sapiens imbues nature through its collective mind with words, names and meaning.

The human mind is the birth-place of reality and, on a higher plane, of abstract existence[*].

By being able to learn and comprehend the language of nature (mathematics!), we were able to analyse and understand some of the inner workings of our physical world. Without human participation, our countless acts of conscious observation and intelligent deduction, the physical world would be less than . . . .

"to be".

However, humans cannot be seen to exist in isolation. From a holistic point of view they are an integral part of the universe and therefore, by realising the universe, **doesn't the universe also realise itself?**

Initially geared to succeed in competitive battles for survival, the human mind, hopefully, will keep on developing, expanding and shaping its own destiny in tandem with the cosmic expansion of our physical world. Hopefully, the strong link with the U-Mind[**] will keep on growing stronger until the glory days in the distant future, the time I call **"Era of fulfillment"**, when cosmic expansion reaches its peak and amplified consciousness will have spread throughout

---

[*]   Next on the agenda of human intellectual endeavours ought to be a full understanding of abstract existence. A great start was made when we realised recently that material reality, in essence, is movement.

[**]   The strong link is obvious. It is bluntly displayed in our creative spirit trying to duplicate and even emulate nature, although still in rather insignificant ways.

the physical world, when superminds in far-flung places unite by means of telepathic conversation in full knowledge of the Universal Mind ....

when the universe will be in dialogue with itself.

However, during the next few decades and beyond, humans have to play, to the best of their ability, their allocated role in the greater scheme. As spearheads of evolution they are equipped with a mind of great potential, but to survive and develop further they have to channel this mind collectively in the right direction. Humankind needs to appreciate the order of the universe, shake off the shackles of impeding culture and divisive, obsessive and destructive religion, overcome racial divisions, introduce reasonable international standards of morality and codes of ethical behaviour and re-introduce punishment that befits the crime but above all, protect the environment and fight the disease of greed and crass materialism.

Presently, conditions for the improvement and further development of the human race are extremely difficult. With a multitude of conflicting ideas and views it is not surprising that most of human kind **still cannot "see" the true purpose of human existence.**

For billions of people the answer concerning the purpose of human existence is based on anti-quated religious beliefs but sadly, for most of the more progressive-minded, the true purpose of human and other intelligent life form's existence is also obscure. A great many people, especially in the western world, are caught in the vortex of modern life. People are born and people die. In between these momentous occasions they grow up, get an education and from this point onward they are fully occupied, alternating between work and leisure but mostly work. Very few question the purpose of human existence and if asked what it may be, the common answers are "there is no real purpose" or "nobody knows for certain". However, if one asks them the purpose of their lives, each answer takes on an individual flair because each person has his or her own views. The answer depends on the individual's mind-set, his or her out-look on life, character and external influences, experiences and circumstances. For example someone may feel that life gives them a chance to work for status or class or to live a life of adventure or pleasure or find fulfilment in the creation of a family, etc. All well, however, most still cannot see the true purpose of human existence.

Is there an actual purpose of universal validity one may ask?

I am convinced that there is!

Raise the level of awareness and discover the exquisite and intricate order of our physical world, recreated from seemingly anarchical conditions at the beginning of our cycle of physical existence. Reflect on nature's unbelievable desire to aim for awe-inspiring balanced levels of excellence and beauty during the expansion phase of our physical world. Contemplate development, in particular evolution and you will notice nature's steady march toward greater complexity culminating in the creation of consciousness and the human mind, a mind which is presently trying to discover and understand the hidden secrets of our universe, a mind which is trying to create what nature creates, **a mind which is trying to read the mind that ultimately created it.**

Yes, the true purpose of human and/or other intelligent life form's existence becomes obvious if we consider that our minds, still feeble and small, **will never cease to strive for fulfilment.**

As long as our physical world expands, our minds, hopefully, will follow suit. The potential exists for mind to expand beyond our imagination and for consciousness to spread throughout the physical world and, in millions of years from now, breaking through the barriers of space and time and **unite with the Universal Mind.**

Yes, dictated by nature itself, the ultimate aim and purpose of human existence is union of the human mind with the Universal Mind.

Reminiscent of a flower's bloom before fading, this could be the culmination of a glorious phase in this cycle of physical existence. Humans could reach the apex of nature's path of development that started with subatomic particles and progressed past atoms and molecules to simple life, followed by more complex life including the development of a brain and the unfolding of mind. The evolution from a self-conscious to an advanced mind and further development to a super mind is all within our reach. **Now, again dictated by nature, the immediate aim and purpose of our existence is to carry the torch of consciousness to ever greater heights.**

Because our survival depends on the survival of balanced nature, we have an obligation to integrate our own needs and (often selfish) aspirations with that of nature to our own and nature's benefit. Go with nature's flow and strive for balanced greatness and a better world and remember, there is no pleasure without pain and no happiness without depression; accept the truth but strive to overcome obstacles in your path. We have less control over our thoughts and feelings than we would like but we have reasonable control over our actions and it is through mindful action that we create a meaningful life.

THE UNIVERSE

Latin: universum, neut. sing. of universus, whole.

Universe means "The Whole System of Things" or "All that is'. It does not specifically imply "the whole system of physical (or material) things". Nevertheless, the word is commonly used to describe the totality of physical things, observed or postulated; in other words, the entire cosmos.

Going back in time to the ancient Greeks, the universe seemed to consist of the Mediterranean Sea and its adjacent land together with a mythical surrounding ocean and overarching sky, a dome, not very far overhead, containing the heavenly bodies. Later it was commonly conceded that the earth was spherical but its size remained a mystery until the voyages of Christopher Columbus and other explorers around 1500 AD. In 1543 a hypothesis was published, written by Nicolaus Copernicus that the earth is only one of several planets revolving around the sun. His work was condemned by the Roman Catholic church and the ban was not lifted until 1758. In opposition to all efforts to discredit him, his theory was gradually accepted and later confirmed by astronomers. It also became evident that the stars were much more remote than had been suspected and they realised that the sun itself was one of the stars. The idea of the solar system being inside the milky way galaxy was suggested by Thomas Wright in 1750 and confirmed by William Herschel late in the 18th century. During the 19th and 20th centuries there were speculations as to whether the milky way galaxy was limited or infinite (constituting the whole universe). Immanuel Kant and Johann Lampert suggested that there were other "island universes" just like our milky way, perhaps infinite in number. Between 1910 and 1925 astronomers discovered convincing evidence that the so-called nebulae outside the milky way were indeed "island universes" or galaxies as these stellar systems are now called.

This is how the universe grew and grew ….

Times have changed and so have human perceptions and their horizon. I have renamed what is commonly known as the universe "physical world" because in my view the universe proper, "the whole system of things", does not only consist of the totality of physical things but is a union of three different, yet complementary worlds. Yes, the universe is a multi-layer, multi-level system, its main components being:

The Physical World(s),
The U-Minded World
The Primordial World

The Physical World's main attributes and properties are:

Three dimensional space and the controversial dimension of time (these are normal dimensions making up "ordinary" space-time). Additional invisible (compactified and internal) dimensions are considered by scientists for diverse applications, for example to accommodate the four forces of nature in string and brane theories.

The physical world's primary substance is Substantia, consisting of Posens, Negens and Neutens. Substantia is accountable for the movements (vibrations, spin and vortex like) and energy of all known elementary particles of matter and forcefields. Restmass and forces are the results of vortexlike inward movements of elementary particles of matter.

Our physical world consists of different, tightly connected levels of existence. Reality (Existence Level "A") is subdivided into classes I, II, III, & IV.

Existence Level "B" is the mental world of homo sapiens and

Existence Level "C" is abstract existence, also sub-divided into different classes.

The U-Minded world's main attributes and properties (relative to our physical world) are:

Wholeness, an entirely different system of being to our own. Wholeness means unbroken, U-minded existence. The system is not governed by the laws of physics but by the U-mind.

U-minded Pos, Neg and Neut are the U-minded world's equivalent counterparts to the physical world's Posens, Negens and Neutens. They are accountable for "U-minded motion-power" named "Potentia", the "subjective" and complementary counterpart ("software") to the physical world's "movement-energy" ("hard-ware").

Particularised "U-minded motion-power" named "Potentia partis" is the nonphysical (Potentia) aspect of an elementary particle's nature. It is the "doorway" leading from the U-minded world to the physical world and vice versa. In any elementary particle, increasing concentration of movement-energy toward the centre stops at a critical point ("long" before the dreaded infinity disease strikes!). At this spot, transmutation of movement-energy to Potentia partis and transubstantiation from either Posens, Negens or Neutens into U-minded Pos, Neg and Neut respectively, occurs. Movements thereafter are not bound by physical restrictions. This mode of existence (wholeness) gives scientists the impression of instant, superluminal (faster than the speed of light) "information transfer" in specific experiments between particles separated by vast distances in space.

U-minded Pos, Neg and Neut are "advanced" (controlled by the U-mind) versions of the primordial, eternally moving Pos, Neg and Neut of Existence Level "Y".

It is in this world, on Existence Level "X", situated between the primordial and the physical world, that the U-mind disposed the laws and rules of nature that guarantee continuity of physical existence.

The Primordial World "occupies" Level "Y", the "most remote" level of existence. Its mode of being (in our terms!) is most refined, insubstantial and "super-idea like" and although our atoms predominately consist of empty space, it is far removed from the coarseness of ordinary space-time.

In this archetypal world as anywhere else, the Absolute is non-existent, but here the reason for its non-existence is glaringly obvious: the Absolute is divided, split into primordial opposites "Pos" and "Neg". Although trying to reunite in agitated surges, primordial Pos and Neg are permanently separated by an equally dynamic "Neut". Pos, Neut and Neg are primary entributes of the first order of existence, named "primordial entributes". Neut in its centre role, permanently forced to move, prevents final re-union of Pos and Neg but also prevents dismemberment by virtue of springlike residual forces that holds them within optimal range. The results of this dynamic arrangement are eternal "forward" and "backward" surges, movements I called "primary-motion power", the "proto" of all movements everywhere. Last but not least, a primordial mind permeates and controls the primordial world, its one-track mind fully set on one purpose:

Existence, balanced existence in fact.

The Universe exists in dependence upon Pos, Neut and Neg, and the non-existence of the absolute.

THE UNIVERSE

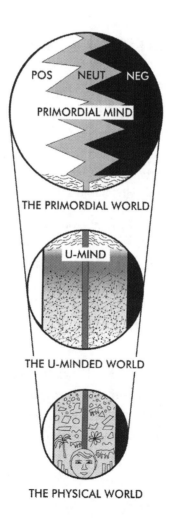

5

THE U-MINDED WORLD

EXISTENCE LEVEL "X"

Although unable to discern, humans will have to accept the truth that the physical world is permeated by an intangible "sea of pure ideas", a realm of possibilities, probabilities and certainties under the regimen of a "supermind" with "super ideas". Yes, the wholeness of the U-minded world is bizarre and, "seen" from our frame of reference, a world of paradox "situated" between the physical world and the primordial world of Existence Level "Y".

From the uncertain behaviour of subatomic particles, their seemingly own decision making ability in certain sets of circumstances, their interconnectedness and apparent ability to communicate whilst disregarding the limitations of space and time, all seen in relation to the unquestionable ingenuity of the natural world, I infer Existence Level "X" to consist of no more than three different main layers of activity

1. **Top Layer:**
    Primary Potentia (Primary U-minded motion-power)* "effecting" the "multi-layer" (space-time is irrelevant in the realm of wholeness) "invention" of the U-minded world as well as the multi-tier "disposal" of all fundamental rules and laws of our physical world.
2. **Middle Layer:**

---

*   Derived from primary motion-power and "remodelled" to U- mind's specification.

Secondary Potentia (secondary U-minded motion-power, "derived" from primary U-minded motion-power), effecting the "control (strict adherence to rules and laws) and maintenance activity" of both, the U-minded and physical worlds via a kind of "communication-computation" (c.-c.) signal* network.

3. **Bottom Layer:**

Potentia partis (border U-minded motion-power), adjoins the physical side of any elementary particle, in fact it is the non-physical aspect of an elementary particle's nature and serves as signal reception and dispatch port.

Due to our lingering inability to understand the operation of the top layer, our attention will be focused mainly on the middle and bottom layers.

What is Potentia?

Foremost, Potentia is the pre-requisite for everything that exists in the physical world and primary Potentia for most of what exists in the U-minded world, but most importantly, Potentia "precedes" movement-energy.

Potentia, the U-minded motion-power is the power to be and to do anything conducive for (optimal) existence and continuity thereof – not in reality, actuality or fact but in possibility, probability and/or certainty.

In essence, U-minded motion-power is an "advanced version" of primary motion-power, one of the inherent effects of the principle of existence on Existence Level "Y". Acclaim for the "improvements" has to go to the U-mind, supremely ruling the wholeness of our neighbouring world.

Signals are transmitted effects, kinds of "particles in idea" and also "moving bits" of movements, fully integrated with other signals and signal ports. Because signals are "moving bits" of movements, the question arises again: "What moves and interacts on this level of existence"? Certainly not anything discernable or tangible and also not "nothing" as some scientists might suggest.

No, the moving and interacting signals are highly disciplined "advanced" versions of the primordial *entributes*" Pos, Neut and Neg, renamed on this

---

* A "transmitted" effect, conveying a message.

level of existence "U-minded" Pos, Neut and Neg. As "U-mind-drenched bits" of fundamental idea, they are the U-minded world's (equivalent) counter parts to the physical worlds Posens, Neutens and Negens (which are primarily accountable for the physical world's movement-energy).

However, the U-minded world's (Pos-Neut -Neg) movements are unlike ordinary space-time bound movements. Although specific movements ascribed to signals and signal reception and dispatch ports are unknown, an infinite number of seemingly erratic, faster than the speed of light signals "criss-cross" the middle layer.

Because of wholeness conditions, any signal by either U-minded Pos, Neut or Neg would be perceived, from our frame of reference, as being "instant". In accordance with my elementary particle – Potentia theory, these seemingly "super-fast moving" signals are "transmitted" effects in a universal Potentia communication-computation "net-work". Every space-time bound particle decision, however insignificant in the greater scheme, in nature or as part of a scientific experiment, is based on results of "instant" communication-computation activity. On our time scale in our frame of reference all communication-computation activities in the U-minded world, simple or complex, last an "instant". Although such result is understandable considering it emerges from an "environment" of wholeness, it still poses a serious mental challenge to our "movements in ordinary space-time" conditioned brain. In addition, human languages evolved by way of everyday experiences within the confines of our physical world. It pains me to have to resort describing the ineffable in terms of two or three spatial dimensions whilst trying to avoid depicting movements in the wholeness of the U-minded world in terms of ordinary time. To adequately describe conditions, "things" and activities as they really are and occur, is at present simply impossible. The U-minded world

is

part of nature but most of it still beyond our understanding. Notwithstanding the fact that many physicists called it or still call it "nothingness" or "hidden dimension" and large sections of the fraternity simply ignore it for lack of empirical evidence, some reputable physicists were convinced that there is more to this "nothingness" than meets the eye. They In fact "knew" of an unbroken realm that exists beyond familiar reality and is more difficult to understand than quantum theory and relativity, they "knew" of **a kind of "wholeness" which seemingly allows faster than the speed of light (superluminal) "information transfer" ("communication-computation signalling" in my theory) between widely separated parts of our physical world.**

This insight was gained by the strange "connectedness" between subatomic particles ("quantum connectedness". See "The Unity of our physical world"). The most prominent pioneers of quantum physics who subscribed to this view were John Bell, a physicist at the "Centre for European nuclear research" (Cern) in Geneva, Switzerland and Professor David Bohm of Birkbeck College, London (see "A Brief History of Quantum Mechanics"). They and other quantum physicists came up with concepts such as "superluminal information transfer", "superluminal quantum connectedness", superluminal transfer of negentropy without signals" and a non-causal connecting principle called "synchronicity". They realised that quantas (naturally fixed minimum amounts of physical energy or plain "sub-atomic particles) are not "things" in the usual sense but more like **"correlated tendencies to happen".**

Quantum scientific experiments have shown that sub-atomic particles are seemingly **"making their own decisions"** but further evidence shows that decisions they seem to make **"depend on particle decisions made elsewhere".**

Sub-atomic particles seem to be instantly aware what decisions are made elsewhere and this can be as far away as another galaxy. Evidence reveals not only **"intimate and immediate particle relations over long distances",** but clearly demonstrates **"particle interdependence".**

Prima facie evidence suggests "faster than the speed of light information transfer" but this seems to be an oversimplification of the true "state of affairs". The only possibility I found reasonable was **the existence of a different system of being, a different world, complementary to our ordinary space-time physical world, a realm that accommodates and facilitates the true fundamental processes of nature without the encumbrance of physical space and time, a realm called**

Wholeness...

But before we mindfully venture into the realm of wholeness, more light needs to be shed on the fascinating topic of Potentia.

POTENTIA

Latin: potens, - entis, pr.p. of posse, to be able.

Derived from the Primordial, the U-mind and Potentia "evolved" in tandem.

Potentia exists, it cannot not exist. Just imagine a universe without Potentia! There would be nothing (well, almost nothing!), not even movement–energy because energy is secondary to Potentia in the order of being; no planets, stars or galaxies, no dark energy nor dark matter, just eerie emptiness. However, if we could "see beyond" we would still discover another world, the primordial world, intangible, insubstantial but "filled" with balanced movements and super-great but idle, unemployed power – the power to be – nothing else!

Yes, without Potentia in the wholeness of a U-minded world, primordial movements would be the only sign of existence.

Three main layers of Existence Level "X" "embody" all that's conducive to "satisfy" U-mind's purpose, aim and direction, **not in reality or fact but in possibility, probability and/or certainty.**

For example, in the top layer of Existence Level "X", the U-mind may have prioritised some possibilities for a specific purpose by means of computation. After "further scrutiny", only one possibility will become a certainty to be used for whatever purpose it was meant to be used for.

Yes, this is how the U-mind "modelled" its own world <u>and</u> disposed the rules and laws of the physical world.

The U-mind and Potentia are the "source" of all (well almost all!) there is.

Potentia is U-minded motion-power. All minded activity is powered by enhanced, inherent movements (details unknown) of Pos, Neut and Neg, however, the exact relationship between U-mind and motion-power will remain a closed book for a long time, remember, humans have not even resolved complexities relating to the interaction between a human brain and the abstract-existent entity of a human mind!.

The scope of U-minded motion-power is limited to within the framework of U-mind's purpose, aim and direction, as for example evidenced in our microcosm where checks and limits are imposed by the laws of conservation and probability. Probability laws exclude much of what the conservation laws permit, but the scope of development within this rigid framework is **endless.....**

You do not need to be a nature lover to be intrigued by the endless beauty, variety and diversity of nature on our planet, all initiated beyond ordinary space and time in the wholeness of the U-minded world.

POTENTIA PARTIS

Unbeknown to most humans, the unobtrusive elementary particle not only seems to be, but actually <u>is</u> the essential link connecting our physical world, more specifically, the outer edge of the microcosm, to the bottom layer of Existence Level "X". "Evidence" seems to corroborate the idea that the elementary particle "incorporates" the point of transition from one state of being to another state, from ordinary space-time to the wholeness of the U-minded world. It is also the point where transubstantiation from physical Substantia (Posens, Neutens and Negens) to U-minded Pos, Neut and Neg, and transmutation from physical movement–energy to U-minded motion-power (Potentia partis) occurs[*].

One could argue that the definition of "elementary particle" is valid only to the point where the two worlds meet, especially if we consider that in "Wholeness-proper" no individual parts exist[**]. Nevertheless, "connections" exist, however intangible, and it is at any of these "connections", extending minimally beyond ordinary space-time ("signal-reception and dispatch ports") where we "find":

Potentia partis.

---

[*] My mental "construction" of an elementary particle suggests increasing vortexlike movement-energy (to a great degree spherical/ball like for particles with mass, flat for particles with no mass) toward the centre, resulting in extremely high energy in extremely small space. At a point well off infinite strength of energy, I visualise the occurrence of transmutation from physical movement-energy to U-minded motion-power (Potentia partis).

[**] Signals and ports are integrated, making up a state of being called "Wholeness".

Potentia partis is part of a whole, intimately connected by integrated middle-layer activity to other Potentia partis.

According to my hypothesis, each and every elementary particle of matter, force fields and the vacuum **"keeps one foot in the U-minded world"**, **meaning, the true nature of an elementary particle is two-sided.**

First and foremost we ought to acknowledge its **physical world-quantum energy aspect,** explored and researched in quantum mechanics, particle physics and associated scientific fields as well as utilised in advanced technology, but "there is more to a particle than meets the eye".

The U-minded world – Potentia aspect (Potentia partis) of an elementary particle's nature is shrouded in the mystery of its so-called "irrationality" but in my view (inspired by the theories of some prominent scientists), it is precisely this absurd behaviour that provides evidence for the existence of a U-minded world. Yes, the irrational aspect of subatomic phenomena provides "proof" that **there ought to exist an "environment" that allows** seemingly supernatural relationships among particles, relationships that do not comply with old established rules and laws of physics and are contrary to our perception of ordinary space and time. For example restrictions imposed on the system of our physical world do not allow anything to move faster than light (300,000 km/sec). After due consideration I concluded that apparent **instant (superluminal)** particle "information transfer" or, now more appropriately worded, "communication-computation signalling" (C.-C. signalling), sometimes across vast stretches of ordinary space, actually occur **outside or beyond** ordinary space-time in the so-called "wholeness of the U-minded world", directly influencing (often extremely odd) particle decisions in any sets of circumstances. It ought to be emphasised that, contrary to conventional thinking, C.-C. signals do not physically travel across space, they are only active within the wholeness of the U-minded world.

Apart from scientific observations and "evidence" revealed by the wave function, what really convinced me of the two-sided nature of elementary particles was the fact that they themselves were the direct and only means to **enable** "instant and intimate relationships" among themselves, even when separated by vast distances.

PARTICLE DECISIONS

Regarding the statement, "Every space-time bound particle decision . . . is based on results of "instant" C.-C. activity", it must be clarified that, firstly, it is not U-mind that induces particle decisions of any kind, not in physical nature nor in scientific experiments. Although U-mind's purpose, direction and laws are fully absorbed in secondary movements (middle layer) of Potentia, it is Potentia partis (bottom layer) that **induces** particle decisions based on results of C.-C. activity (middle layer), directly contributing to a kind of

UNIVERSAL CONSCIOUSNESS.

However, Potentia partis, being the U-minded world aspect of an elementary particles' nature, **cannot effect** decisions, it can only induce them by impelling the physical side to carry the decision into effect.

POTENTIA PARTIS AND PARTICLE-UNCERTAINTY

Potentia partis is the U-minded world aspect of an elementary particle's nature. This has to have an immediate effect on the physical aspect. Yes, the proximity of an entirely different world with different mode of being "brings about" the uncertain particle behaviour witnessed by quantum physicists.

What is particle-uncertainty?

In classical/Newtonian physics we can determine both, the position and the momentum of an object moving through space at a particular time. From this we are able to calculate where it will be at a specific time in the future. Both these rules do not apply to subatomic particles.

In 1925, the German physicist Werner Heisenberg discovered that if he "zooms in" on a particle's position, he cannot determine with equal precision its momentum and if he measures its momentum, its exact position is lost. Now, if a particle cannot have a position and a momentum at the same time we cannot sensibly ascribe to it a path through space, in fact, experiments have shown that a particle, in getting from A to B seems to **"pursue all possible paths at once!"**

In 1927, particle-uncertainty became a central tenet of the "Copenhagen interpretation of quantum mechanics".

Why does Potentia partis cause such behaviour? In my view, Potentia partis induces a particle decision based on incoming result of complex C.-C. signal network operations, after sending a message of impending decision-making to the middle layer, all this at an instant on our scale of time. The incredible speed of delivery is only possible because of wholeness, the very special state of being beyond the borders of our physical world.

In the middle layer "environment" where a decision (most of the time insignificant!) depends on momentary circumstances and conditions of (probably) "topic related" network of activity, **nothing is absolutely certain** from present to present; everything is in flux until the very instant Potentia partis receives a signal to induce the decision by impelling the physical side to carry the decision into effect.

The uncertainty "filters" through into ordinary space-time to the complementary, physical aspect of a particle's nature (hence its "fuzziness").

The degree to which a particle "feels" its way from a straight line on its way from A to B is determined by its physical mass. A heavier particle keeps more to a straight line. This evidence suggests that increased mass/energy reduces the "scope" of possible paths, its course becomes more certain although it keeps its general "fuzziness".

Particle uncertainty rules out any chance of accurately forecasting specific events but quantum mechanics can accurately predict **probabilities.**

Because we can never know "what a particle decides" at the last moment before an observation or measurement, quantum mechanics can only predict the odds (likelihood) of a definite result or "event" to occur. It can foretell how a group of particles will behave but of an individual particle the only thing it can predict is how it will probably behave.

How can physicists predict the probability of a definite result if they don't know "what a particle decides" at the last moment?

The answer is quite simple. In any quantum mechanical experiment, the particle in question is –"**harnesssed**".

One of the preconditions of an experiment is that the experiment must be properly prepared and rigidly set up. Only after stringent preparations is the scientist able to translate all the specifications of the experimental arrangement into mathematical language. The physicist could never calculate probabilities unless he knows all the initial conditions of the experiment. Included in these specifications are sections, each one corresponding to a different **possible** result or "event" to occur. In "classical procedure" the mathematical quantities are then fed into Erwin Schrödinger's wave equation. This is one of the most famous equations of physics, ranking with Einstein's $E = mc^2$ but more complex. It expresses the form of natural causal development of a raw state, Group 2, Type "A" particle, for example "travelling" from A, its source (the region of preparation) to B, the region of measurement or observation. While moving from A to B, a dynamic ("wavelike") unfolding of all specified possibilities occurs according to Schrödinger's wave equation.

This **"development of possibilities"** is represented by a particular kind of mathematical entity that not only has the status of "central mathematical element" of Schrödinger's equation but of quantum mechanics as a whole. He called it **"wave function"** because it encapsulates mathematically the complementary aspect of all particles in motion – a developing wave. The form of the wave function can be calculated for any moment between the particle's exit from its source A to the moment of interaction at B. Squaring the wave function's amplitude results in the creation of the **"probability (density) function"**.

It tells the scientist the probabilities at any given time of each of the possibilities represented by the wave function. Scientists are thus able to predict the probability of a result or event but **not the result or event itself.**

Which possibility becomes an actuality may appear to be a matter of pure chance but appearances are known to deceive. From my point of view, which possibility becomes an actuality is definitely not a matter of absolutely pure chance, even in "straight jacket" experimental conditions. I infer this as a logical conclusion from studying facts of quantum physics and from considerations of scientific and philosophical views of leading physicists. My view is that any decision made by the physical side of a particle was induced by Potentia partis based on results of C.- C. activity in the middle layer of Existence Level "X".

As soon as the scientist makes an observation or measurement, one of the specified possibilities becomes an actuality, for example in the form of a trace on a photographic plate. The trace reveals distinguishing characteristics (for example mass, spin and charge) of specific particles. **Quantum mechanics stipulates that a particle in its raw state, before an interaction, observation or measurement (before wave function collapse) is not really a particle but a tiny, fuzzy field (or blob) of energy and, according to the wave function, in abstract terms, a developing, multifaceted potentiality.**

I categorised this type of particle as belonging to Group 2, type "A".

In high energy particle physics, particles are annihilated and new one's created in experimental collisions. The new (known and sometimes unknown) particles are created from the kinetic energy of the projectile particle and the mass-energy of the target particle. My interpretation of an experimental particle collision is as follows:

During the high energy crunch, the media of movements (either Posens, Neutens or Negens) and, as a consequence, the movements of the particles undergo a kind of "sorting" in the "shortlived broth" (of substantia) before new particles emerge, the result solely depending on related Potentia activity in the U-minded world and the amount of energy and kinds of particles involved in the physical world. Experiments like these clearly demonstrate that a particle **potentially** exists as a combination of other particles, however, on the physical/mathematical plane it is the wave function that, in a very conspicuous manner, clearly points to the power that exists beyond our horizon, patronising the fringes of space-time – **Potentia.**

Potentia and energy collectively, and Potentia partis and particle energy individually, exist "side by side" in different worlds as complementary partners in our universe.

WHOLENESS

Sometimes truth is stranger than fiction and nowhere in the physical world is this more pronounced than in the subatomic realm. Here, paradoxes abound and, as we stated previously, one of the most intriguing aspects of quantum science is the fact that scientists are unable to "pin down" the fundamental building blocks of matter, radiation and forces. The inability to acknowledge subatomic particles as "fully fledged" physical entities sends out an important message: "humans have to accept and live with the fact that "deep down", on a very small scale, reality is anything but real. It is therefore not surprising that, in our endeavour to analyse and describe the state of wholeness, we are forced to deal with difficulties of expression and contradictions. The main reason for this is the difference in the system of Being between the physical and the U-minded world, in human terms comparable to something existing in reality and something bizarre, existing in idea only. Unlike our experience of everyday life (the hustle and bustle of our physical world), U-minded wholeness projects an image of "ethereal insubstantiality", however, considering the "ghostliness" of subatomic particles and conditions at the frontiers of empirical knowledge in general, such vision has to be admitted as being a true reflection of this particular state of being.

What is wholeness?

Wholeness is not "oneness". The word originates from old English "hal" meaning healthy and from old norse "heill" meaning unbroken, healthy and unhurt. In our context "wholeness" means **unbroken, U-minded existence.**

With painfully limited vision I imagine the state of wholeness to be an intangible weblike system with infinite numbers of superfine connections joining every single elementary particle in our physical world. Connections "start" and "end" at ports ("regions" of Potentia partis adjoining the physical "side" of a particle) with no space as we know, in between. An infinite number of instant C.-C. signals (transmitted effects comprising, in whatever "form", U-minded Pos, Neut and Neg) "criss-cross" the middle layer of the U-minded world, in effect "creating" a kind of "universal consciousness". For example, if a Potentia partis receives a signal requesting a particle decision, related middle layer C.-C. signal activity will most certainly ensure the induction of a sensible particle decision via same Potentia partis, all at an instant in our frame of reference. Multiply this by the total of required particle decisions (mostly routine decisions) in our physical world at any one moment, and we get an idea of the scope of activity in the middle layer of the U-minded world.

"Abuzz" with signals only, this supersensible world has no obvious forward (nor backward) movement of time and, as a consequence, no future and no past as we know. The notion of time arises from changes observed and experienced in our physical world but there cannot be changes to any one signal nor can there be signal changes (to change means to alter or make different) as each signal is an instantly transmitted effect requiring no measurable time nor change of position and nobody can nor does measure recurrence in physical terms. However, there is a kind of memory, a power to "retain" important impressions, "located" in the top layer. All the rules and laws of nature are "stored" in "memory" to "secure" repetitions of our cycle of physical existence as well as to "create" a kind of general consciousness (signal and impression related only) incorporating the past, present and future of our physical world, from cycle to cycle to cycle . . . , a "painting" of our physical existence. In contrast, the universal consciousness "created" in the middle layer, (again signal and impression related only), only covers a present moment, a momentary part of the unfolding of events with the flow of time, a narrow strip on the painting of our physical existence. Interaction between the top and middle layers cannot be inferred but common sense tells me to assume they exist.

It is not impossible that the U-minded world is still developing over an unknown measure of time, its flow of time completely unrelated to our cosmic flow. As this is pure speculation I shall maintain the tenet of "no space nor time as we know" regards the U-minded world.

How is such existence possible?

We know that a space and timeless "nothing" cannot ever be said to exist because it is a negation of existence. On the other hand, could a state of being without space and time as we know be possible? Could such a state exist? I maintain it can.

I named the concepts of space and time (as postulated by, among others, Isaac Newton and later modified by Albert Einstein) "ordinary" space-time. Isaac Newton regarded all of space as having a positive, objective existence, not dependent upon subjective conditions of the mind. The physical world was reduced to simple concepts such "displacements in space and persistence in time".

All this changed in the twentieth century. In modern physics a body in motion is considered as carrying along with it a space that is essentially distinct from the space with reference to which it is in motion.

In Einstein's special theory of relativity, the speed of light is the only universal constant and everything in the physical world, including space and time, is related to this speed.

This theory, verified by many minor experiments, led to incredible conclusions.

Concerning space:

From a stationary observer's frame of reference, a moving object measures shorter in its direction of motion as its speed increases until, at the speed of light, it disappears.

Concerning time:

From a stationary observer's frame of reference a moving clock runs more slowly as its speed increases until, at the speed of light, it stops running altogether,

Concerning mass:

From a stationary observer's frame of reference, the mass of a moving object measures more as its speed increases until, at the speed of light, it becomes infinite.

Supposing a man departed aboard a space-craft to some distant destination in space. Steadily increasing the speed of his craft he then travels at close to the speed of light. After several years he returns to our planet only to find that he was away for centuries of earth time.

This scenario is not any more science fiction, it could be for real.

Relative to a stationary observer, a body moving at the speed of light is just not there! Its space and time has ceased to be part of reality. Movements faster than the speed of light are not possible in **ordinary space-time.**

The neutrino, one of the strangest of sub-atomic particles and said to be travelling at the speed of light, is almost completely oblivious of solid matter. It could penetrate several light-years thickness of solid lead and apart from being (so far!) the most common entity in space, comes closest to being - "pure nothing!!".

The neutrino, the photon (particle of light!) and the "elusive graviton" carry no mass, electric charge and move at the speed of light. From a stationary observer's frame of reference their intrinsic selves are nothing but movement-energy, moving movements (from a physics point of view, their only property is a kind of spin) or movements in motion!

We know that if a scientist measures a particle's momentum, it is impossible for him to zoom in on its position and vice-versa. At that level, space, time, geometry and physical being in general have, from a scientist's point of view, become problematic.

Albert Einstein told us that our physical world is space-time activity, that space can stretch, shrink, bend and distort. Just as the uncertainty principle fuzzes out the activity and geometry of particles, space-time on the quantum level becomes foamy in structure (this is based on results of mathematical modelling). The results show violent, impulsive growth and decay of curvature of space and space itself is made up of an infinite number of ghost spaces (bubbles!). Again the concepts of locations and geometry in general are lost in the nebulous activity of quantum space-time.

Now, if at the fringes of our physical world space itself becomes obscure and the theory of relativity (supported by empirical evidence) tells us that from a stationary observer's frame of reference an object travelling at the speed of light disappears altogether, should we assume that wholeness equates to space-timelessness? We cannot assume nor can we outright infer because we don't know true conditions in the wholeness of the U-minded world. However, it is obvious that conditions resembling a state of space-timelessness do exist because effects, clearly emanating from beyond the physical horizon, bear testimony to it.

But isn't such Being paradoxical in terms of movements? Isn't it absurd to ascribe motion/ movements to a seemingly space and timeless world? Yes, one of my principle statements says: "Potentia is U-minded motion-power";

another refers to signals as "moving bits of movements not unlike subatomic particles" etc.

In the physical world motion/movements are understood to be acts of changing place or positions in time, but in wholeness, places, positions and time as we know, do not exist. Nevertheless, I still let it be known that movement-activity is the "heart and soul" of wholeness. How do we reconcile this and how do we justify still using the words motion/movements?

It is important to remember that in the U-minded world <u>objective</u> changes are not possible because of the absence of places or positions. Therefore, movements in the U-minded world have to be conceived to be subjective, idea-like and - instant. However, an effect (or multiple effects) lasting an instant in our frame of reference may be stretched to the equivalent of an hour in the wholeness frame of reference, we simply do not know. But we do know that even in our physical world, from a stationary observer's frame of reference, there is no universal space and time, only "proper" (his own) and relative.

Instantaneousness of movements, signals or effects comply with the theories of "superluminal particle information transfer" proposed by well-known quantum physicists. The word "instant" has no connotation to an exact "rate of motion" (distance per unit of time), nevertheless it embraces our concept of time because time not only refers to "stretch of duration" but also to "an instant" (a moment or point of time) in which "things happen", regardless of how short it may be in our frame of reference.

As for the word "movement": for lack of a suitable alternative word signifying subjective, instant and wholeness-appropriate movement, I shall carry on using the illustrative word "movement".

Yes, from a far from perfect human point of view, only freedom from the shackles of space and time can assure what I define as **true Wholeness.**

As conceived in our frame of reference, there is no space nor flow of time from instant to instant, no future and no past as we know in the wholeness of the U-minded world, only an infinite number of movements, each in it's present time.

PART TWO

PRIMARY FACTORS IN HUMAN EXISTENCE

6

ETHICS

THE PRINCIPLE

Human history is filled with conflicts ranging from personal battles to warfare involving nations and continents, but now, in the twenty-first century, we are facing manmade problems that actually threaten our survival as a species. The excessive decimation of unspoilt nature in the name of progress and unchecked population growth in underdeveloped countries combined with unrestrained migration into cities and shantytowns are the maincauses that gravely upset the balance of nature. In addition, we experience excessive greed, extreme materialism and increasing crime, especially in the western world, re-emerging religious fanaticism, political/religious polarisation with threats of mass destruction but, most importantly, a deep **moral crisis** generated by the clash between modern, progressive, less religious, more scientific but often far too liberal minded people on one side, and followers of antiquated "stuck in the mud" organised religions, out-dated cultural value and belief systems and archaic political ideologies on the other side. Although both sides have snippets of truth and value, the overall result is confusion, dangerous confusion about what is right and wrong, good and bad. Humans need to change. Charles Darwin said: "it is not the strongest of the species that survives, nor the most intelligent, but the one most responsive to change". The present extremely unhealthy situation justifies the urgent introduction (and later step by step implementation) of an **ethical principle of universal value,** by which all human conduct is influenced and, to a greater or lesser extent, controlled, independent of any existing religious or political orientation. The pertinent question is: what is the criterion on which to base a principle of such magnitude?

After long and due consideration I concluded that under almost all conditions and circumstances it is the "Experience of Living" that is "desired" first and foremost, consciously and inherently by almost all humankind, and instinctively or by nature by all fauna and flora.

Yes, there is a primary, "innate desire" to live and, depending on circumstances, a more or less strong secondary "innate desire" to improve the quality of life, in all of living nature.

In humans this "innate desire" to live (or "the will to live" as it is generally known) is most pronounced in life-threatening situations. Things of material value are temporarily forgotten, highly esteemed and great ideals such as "the pursuit of happiness" are temporarily erased from one's mind*.

Only a minority of the human population on our planet do not care if they were dead or alive and even less wish they were dead, for example deeply depressed, mentally disturbed and unstable people or someone suffering incredible physical pain with no hope of improvement. Also indoctrinated promises of a martyr's paradise may persuade potential suicide bombers to give up their lives, but otherwise the strong "innate desire" and "naked will" to survive and **to live is prevalent. Therefore, life and the experience of living is of primary value to humankind.**

There is no doubt that a good quality, balanced life and preservation of such life until it's natural end is the criterion on which to base the ethical principle of universal value. It reads as follows:

A balanced and good quality Life is innately and ought to be consciously of primary value to all humankind. Therefore, in the scheme of human existence all human activities and actions ought to be done in the spirit of achievement and preservation of such life.

Living a balanced and good quality life as best as circumstances allow, brings us in tune with greater nature, our universe and the principle on which existence is based.

---

*   However, immediately after subsidence of a life-threatening situation, the "desire" to improve, to a greater or lesser extent, returns.

MORAL OBLIGATION

Yes, the greatest, most valuable gift humans can wish for is a balanced, good quality life, a balanced life style and a bright future for all.

Unfortunately, humankind is stuck in an unprecedented quagmire of extremely serious problems and unless we mend our ways, as individuals and as a society, we will not have much of a future to look forward to. Nobody likes to suffer or live in misery. There is no alternative, we have a **universal, moral obligation** to reconsider our morality and ways of life on all levels of society, be they personal, social, economical, political and religious. We have to acknowledge our failings and mistakes in bold language regardless of strong reactions from the unjustified privileged and powerful, the super rich, the political extreme far left and extreme far right, from dictators, bureaucrats, theocrats and all those who think they are above those living to the golden rule. We have to shed antiquated, destructive ideals hiding behind the cloak of goodness as well as new, extreme-liberal views, crass materialism and ignorance of the value of unspoilt nature, however, keep and re-use anything of value, anything that is genuinely constructive (there is still an abundance of it!).

On a personal level, we have a moral obligation to live a reasonably balanced life, have integrity, follow a reasonably strict moral code of conduct (sexual and otherwise) and have a genuine concern for our fellow humans and the preservation of other forms of life. Indispensible is moderation in activities connected with daily life, including extreme competitive sport (stress can be destructive). The ideal way of life is **a life of reasonable moderation with an obliquity (bias) toward everything positive and constructive.**

Many people would deny this (mostly young!), but a balanced, reasonably conservative, not over-stressed nor boring life style brings forth more contentment and happiness than a life of abundance. Studies have shown that abundance and the quest for ever greater excitement and/or wealth creates a higher degree of restlessness followed by inner emptiness. Also, living a reasonably moderate, balanced life brings us in line with the present positive, developing phase of our cycle of physical existence (incorporating cosmic expansion with the attendant preponderance of general development over degeneration).

Go with the flow!

Reminiscent of a mathematical equation, acceptance of and compliance to the ethical principle as well as adherence to the inferred guidelines does not only achieve optimal conditions for successful living but also provides solid foundations for the survival and further development of humankind. It increases effectively the chances for a successful long-term push towards the "Era of Fulfilment".

A strong, invisible link connects the inventive, creative human mind to the "super-ingenious" U-mind. Acceptance of the ethical principle and adherence to its relevant guidelines, mindful actions, persistent finetuning of human feelings combined with temperance of emotions and passions and a steady increase of knowledge and wisdom are the ingredients for further cohesion of this natural bond during (and in compliance with) the expansionary, developing phase of the present cycle of physical existence.

Yes, given the right conditions and proper guidance, the human mind will carry on striving to ever greater heights and hopefully, in millions of years from now, fulfil its ultimate aim and purpose:

Unity with the Universal Mind.

THE COMMANDMENTS

THE GOLDEN RULE

> *Do not do to others what you would not like done to yourself.*

PRECEPTS

1. Preserve our planet, our natural vegetation, our wildlife and natural resources. They are foundations to our survival and well-being.

2. Live a balanced life, it is the foundation of lasting success. Imbalance leads to unhappiness, depression and destruction. Also, do not esteem excessive riches, fame and power; avoid radicalism and condemn extremism and fanaticism.

3. Keep marriage in very high esteem. In your effort to succeed you will have to compromise. Keep your family small but strong.
Your family is Priority No. 1. Members of your family are more important than your friends.
Guide your children along a balanced path. Do not indoctrinate them unless it is universally right and good. Teach them how to think for themselves, how to evaluate evidence and how to disagree with you. Gain their confidence.
And to children: "honour your father and your mother".

4. Do not commit adultery, incest, rape or sex involving animals.
Abstain from dangerous and risky sexual conduct, however, enjoy your sex life in private. Make sure it does not harm anybody emotionally or physically, potentially or otherwise. Leave others to enjoy their sex life in private whatever their inclinations (which are none of your business).

5. Do not murder a fellow human being nor cause needless harm or suffering to any human or animal, large or small. Do not kill a human being unless it is the last resort in defence of

    a) your country,
    b) yours or
    c) a fellow human's life.

6. Do not steal. Do not be deceptive, corrupt, a liar and a fraud. Also, do not be greedy, cruel, hateful, malicious, overly arrogant and delusional.

7. Do not oppress or discriminate on the basis of sex, race or ethnicity.

8. Do not be a slave to your lower instincts and emotions.
   Do not associate with evil people and bad friends. Drink only alcohol in moderation; if you can't, abstain. Keep your hands off harmful drugs, including cigarettes.
   Beware of gambling. Gambling addiction can have dire consequences. Do not dwell on the negative, macabre, morbid and destructive, instead be positive and constructive.

9. Do not spend more than you earn. Easy credit and loans are seductive.

10. Do not over-crave variety, sensations, change and quick results. Mental unrest leads to distress.

11. Do not overlook evil or shrink from administering justice but always be ready to forgive wrongdoing freely admitted and honestly regretted.

12. Treat your fellow human beings with respect, consideration, politeness, sincerity, kindness and, whenever possible, with generosity; show gratitude towards a benefactor and compassion for the sufferings of other beings.

13. Believe in free speech and protect it even if you disagree with what is being said, however, be sensitive to the sensibilities of others. Insults play no part in free speech.

14. Acquire a good education and satisfying profession/employment/ business/enterprise/ entrepreneurship/vocation.

15. Live life with a sense of joy and wonder, always seek to be learning something new.

16. If possible, test all things, always check your ideas against facts and be ready to discard even a cherished belief if it does not conform to them.

17. Never seek to censor or cut yourself off from dissent (differences of opinion), always respect the right of others to disagree with you.

18. Do not allow yourself to be led blindly by others. Form independent opinions on the basis of your own reason and experience.

19. Pause often, think deeply and question everything.

MIND POWER

You may wonder what the relationship is between ethics, the branch of philosophy which is concerned with human character and conduct – and the power of mind. Well, the best way to effect amelioration of human conduct and improvement of body and mind is by way of the power of mind.

Almost every adult person alive today carries "at the back of his or her mind", in the subconscious and the unconscious, a load of mental garbage affecting, to a greater or lesser extent, his whole life and outlook on life. Often unbeknown to him or her, this garbage has been piling up since childhood. Adverse suggestions and the implanting of negative ideas, information, instructions and comments by parents, friends, teachers and preachers and later by the media can have very negative effects. Important instructions, in many instances taught by "well meaning" educators or religious teachers, may have amounted to no less than systematic, irrational indoctrination. This is of special relevance today because religious irrationality, intolerance and fanaticism seem to have become (again) as much of a threat to world peace as power politics.

Yes, ideas, good or bad, deeply impressed into the unconscious by means of repetitive commands and suggestions/auto-suggestions become powerful forces in people's minds, forces that are able to push them towards success, mediocrity or failure.

The following brief summary of the work of the great pioneer of positive suggestion/ auto-suggestion, Emile Coué, ought to inspire us to use the power of mind in the pursuit of creating a better world.

SUGGESTION – AUTO SUGGESTION

Suggestion – auto-suggestion has been with us since time immemorial but it is only during the last one hundred and fifty years that the immense power of the mind, expressed in suggestion and auto- suggestion, has been properly studied.

The books "Self-mastery" and "The practice of auto-suggestion" by Emile Coué were first published in 1922. They became an immediate success and were re-printed more than sixteen times. Born in 1857 at Troyes, France, Emile Coué practiced as a chemist for nearly thirty years. During this time he became increasingly interested in the healing powers of the mind. In 1910, he opened a clinic at Nancy where he treated patients free of charge. His reputation spread by his successful cures and by a theoretical study of his work by Professor Charles Baudouin, "Suggestion and auto-suggestion". Before he died in 1926, he was one of the most popular practitioners of intangible healing in France.

In his analysis of the human mind, he speaks of two absolutely distinct Selves within us, the conscious and the unconscious. The unconscious Self presides not only over the functions of our organism, but also over all our actions, whatever they may be.

He assures us that our so-called free "will"* in fact is anything but free. It always yields to the "imagination"** that stems from the unconscious. If you "imagine" you cannot finish a task, your will is powerless to make you do it.

You can only succeed by learning to guide your "imagination".

Coué then explained that suggestion (the act of imposing an idea on the brain of another human being) does not work unless suggestion transforms itself into autosuggestion on the part of the receiver (the receiver himself implants the idea into himself). If he does not transform the suggestion into an autosuggestion, it produces no results.

Autosuggestions, firmly implanted in the unconscious, have shaped our lives almost from day one, often to our detriment. Coué intended to change all this ignorance-fuelled fatalism and indeed, he succeeded admirably.

The way to a successful and happy life involved the process of carefully weighing up in your mind the things which are to be the objects of your autosuggestion. Do not wish the impossible. Thereafter repeat several times without thinking of anything else: "this thing is going to happen" or "this thing is going away, etc., etc. ..." Once the unconscious accepts the auto-suggestion, it becomes part of your "imagination". Do not expect instant results. Be patient and the thing or things are realised in every detail.

---

*   The term "will" Is ambiguous, what is probably meant is the "effort of will" (explanation by C. Harry Brooks).

**   The term "imagination" is not wholly appropriate. Rather interpret it as inner "thought" (explanation by C. Harry Brooks). My own interpretation is "inner conviction or "belief".

If you "imagine" that you cannot do the simplest thing in the world, it is impossible for you to do it. Molehills become mountains.

He assures us that because the unconscious is the source of many of our ills, it can also bring about their cure.

But not only can it repair the ill it has done, it's action upon our organism is so strong that it can cure ailments that were dormant since birth. However, he emphasises that it is of major importance that **the "will" must not be brought into play in practising auto-suggestion,** because if the "will" is not in agreement with the "imagination" (saying "you are willing it but it is not going to happen"), not only does one not obtain what one wants, but the exact reverse is brought about.

From daily experiments over twenty years, he was able to formulate the following laws:

1. When the will and the "imagination" are antagonistic, it is always the "imagination" which wins, without exception.
2. When the will and the "imagination" are in agreement, one seems not to add to the other, but rather multiply by the other.
3. The "imagination" can be directed.

Coué then gives another useful advice before starting autosuggestion: realise that it is impossible to think of two things at once, two ideas can be placed side by side but they cannot be superimposed in our mind. One thought at a time entirely filling your mind becomes true and tends to transform into action.

In his clinic at Nancy, Coué acted as indirect healer. His suggestions were transformed by the patient into auto-suggestion, his firm words became part of the patient's "imagination" securely tucked away in the unconscious.

The enormous power yielded by the "imagination" becomes clear when an idea becomes reality, when a sick person becomes healthy, a kleptomaniac ceases to steal, physical pain disappears, etc., etc.... Coué's method of procedure in curative suggestion are longwinded, elaborate and his suggestions border on hypnotism but he emphasises that he does not put his patients to sleep, he only makes them drowsy so that they think of nothing in particular. At the end of the session, he counts to three and the patients open their eyes, smiling. These sessions may have to be repeated but before he sends them away he gives the following instructions: "every morning before rising and every night before sleeping you have to transport yourselves in thought into his presence and then repeat twenty times consecutively in a monotonous voice:

Every day, in every way, I am getting better and better, say it loud (audible to your own ear), simply and with no effort!

For children with health or conduct problems he had a simple treatment: the parents should wait until the child is asleep, then one of them should enter the child's room with precaution, stop a meter in front of it's bed and repeat fifteen to twenty times in murmuring voice all the things they wish to obtain from the child. The parent should then retreat as he or she came in, taking great care not to awake the child.

Never, on any account say to a child "you are lazy and incompetent" because that may give birth to the very faults of which you accuse him or her.

By the powers of the unconscious you will obtain what you want, as long as it is within reason.

Autosuggestion is not a substitute for medical practice. It will not free us from all the common ills of life. They should go hand in hand, each supplementing the other.

During Coué's many years of practising induced autosuggestion in which many thousands of patients were successfully treated, he found that bodily derangements are not harder to treat than nervous or mental ones.

Coué's method of induced autosuggestion was an improvement to hypnotic suggestion which he practised before. It is more simple, more lasting and more universal. The effects of hypnotism are often lost within a few hours after treatment and the most important advantage about autosuggestion: **you do not need a person to suggest if you feel you are sufficiently confident.**

As a practitioner, Coué was a master of his craft, however, I find his idea of "two distinct selves within us" in his analysis of the human mind extremely ambiguous. It could easily be misconstrued as saying that a person has two different minds, a conscious and an unconscious mind. (**For my views see HUMAN MIND**).

Theories on mind, the subconscious and the unconscious are still controversial and will remain so until more light is shed on key-functions of the human brain, for example the precise locations and method of memory impression coding as well as the method of short and long-term memory recall. This, hopefully, would result in the obliteration of the presently popular but controversial terms "the Subconscious" and "the Unconscious".

Since the pioneering days of Emile Coué, teachers and authors of mind-power have mushroomed and so have practitioners of autosuggestion. You find them in all walks of life, from participants in competitive sport to overstressed housewives. In some instances the word autosuggestion has been replaced with the more fashionable term "affirmation" and additional subjects such as visualisation, seeding, intuition, dreams and others have been included in the practice of mind power. However, of all these additions I find only "visualisation", to be of major practical importance. I personally can vouch to the great power of visualisation – imagination as I have imagined one day to be doing what I do now (at the age of seventy years!), fifty-two years ago. Ever since the tender age of eighteen I have searched for answers to the questions of "existence" but everyday-life put a spanner into my works. I had to wait for my retirement before I could seriously consider putting pen to paper.

Today, commercial advertising is making extensive use of the power of suggestion-autosuggestion by means of radio and television. Their marketing technic, in too many cases noisy, repetitive and devoid of any intelligence, must be extremely successful as evidenced by the high number of people seduced to spend more than they earn. In view of this success, why do we not also use the media, but in more constructive ways and for a better purpose such as, for example, steering humankind away from paths of self-destruction?

SUGGESTION-AUTOSUGGESTION IN UNIVERSAL MORAL REGENERATION

Humanity has now reached the stage where important international decisions have to be taken, not only in terms of international relations but also in terms of moral regeneration. A worldwide moral regeneration crusade is not only desirable but an utmost necessity. However, a venture of such magnitude can only be started off by a special branch of an international organisation such as the United Nations because one of the pre-requisites for such a movement has to be full independence from any national, cultural, ethnic or religious ties, interests or ideologies. Their fundamental guide will be the ethical principle of universal value, and their guidelines, if not directly taken over, ought to be based on the commandments. Because the universal moral regeneration will serve humanity as a whole and not only individual interests, it ought to be possible to spread its message by representatives of the United Nations organisation to every corner of our planet. Moral guidance will be broadcast from the aligned nation's media or sent via the worldwide web, and the manner of broadcast (daily repetitions similar to commercial advertising) ought to emphasise the importance of its content. This systematic use of the suggestion-autosuggestion technic is fully justified in view of the fact that its central element is improvement of the quality and the ultimate survival of the human race. Financial funding for this project would have to come from all member nations with contributions depending on size and GDP of each member state.

SUGGESTION-AUTOSUGGESTION IN PARENTHOOD

Family is the foundation of society and the moral health of a nation (and of society as a whole) depends to a great extent on the structure and moral health of its families.

Of all the stages in the life of a human being, the time spent as an active parent are unquestionably the most challenging and most responsible. In addition to looking after the physical wellbeing of a child, a parent has the very important task of fine-tuning its growing mind. A child is very sensitive to suggestions. Without being explicitly told or taught by an expert, a young parent has no idea just how powerful his or her words and deeds are. Positive or negative suggestions transformed by the child into auto-suggestion will influence the course of its life. Always be on your guard what you tell your child, how you tell your child and in your actions teach a child by good example. Tell positive suggestions in a gentle, cheerful tone and repeat them over and over again. When you give a command, try to be even tempered and regulate the tone of your voice to firm but not harsh. Under no circumstances ever be brutal or cruel toward your children and never tell them "you are lazy, naughty, stupid, horrible or good for nothing" because they may later in life just turn out that way. Praise and commend your child often with the words "well done". Instil a sense of curiosity and a desire to know the reason of things. Try to answer all questions, but do not lie. Instead of telling a lie, be rather evasive or at worst tell the child that he or she is still too young to understand. Questions of a sexual nature have to be answered truthfully in a way appropriate to the child's age and maturity of mind. As this is a very sensitive and delicate subject, a reputable book may help you in your task.

Do not unnecessarily implant anxiety and fear in a child's mind by telling bedside stories and fairy tales containing bad witches, wolves and hobgoblins.

Awaken in a child's mind a love for nature, plants and animals and a desire to create, build and construct. Instil a sense of responsibility by explaining the value of study and importance of work.

Impress in his or her mind the very grave danger of associating with bad people, friends and questionable members of the opposite sex. In a surprisingly short time they can brainwash all the good implanted in your child's mind and replace it with their own evil ideas. If possible, keep an eye on them at all times, especially at children's parties; discreetly, so as not to loose their trust and confidence.

Impress in their minds the value of a healthy life-style, not only in words but also in deeds. Always have vegetables as part of your meal, avoid bad fat and keep fruit on the table. Make them or let them participate in as much active sport and outdoor activities as their busy study schedule allows. Prioritise health in general and put illness into the background, but above all, educate them to live a balanced life and avoid life threatening extremes, whatever they may be.

Build a strong self-image. Tell your child you are unique, special and you can do anything you want to do (or have to do) if you really put your mind to it, whether it is at school, in sport or other activities. You have unlimited power to do what has to be done, as well as what you desire or aspire.

Suggestions like these will plant in your child's mind the seeds of self-confidence which is essential for future success and greatness. However, also tell him or her the pitfalls of impulsive actions and over-confidence. Teach your child to use reason before embarking on anything.

To a parent, everyday life in today's information age is very demanding. Tell your child not to believe everything he or she hears, sees or reads. Tell them to question everything and use rational thought to judge or decide upon anything. Keep an eye on the content of their personal means of information but again, be discreet so as not to loose their trust and confidence. Explain to them that a parent has a duty to look after their wellbeing and that it is for their own benefit later in life.

At some stage in life, every normal child may develop feelings of depression or even despair. Sometimes it may just feel down and at other times it may be mentally exhausted, often accompanied by a minor ailment. If this occurs, be especially attentive and show compassion because the problem may loom large in a child's mind. In times of crisis, positive suggestions are of immeasurable value. Tell your child that the problem is not as severe as it seems, there is always a way out, or circumstances will change for the better in due course, etc. etc. Yes, always find words to uplift your child and furnish it with joyous and encouraging thoughts and ideas but always remember, the greatest gift parents can give their children at any time in their lives, in sickness or in health, is to teach them the following auto-suggestion:

Every day, in every way, I am getting better and better ….

For best results let them repeat the sentence twenty times every day in the morning after waking up and in the evening before falling asleep. Tell them <u>not</u> to let the "effort of will" play a role, only the idea. This is important as the inclusion of "will" is counter-productive until the auto-suggestion is fully impressed in their unconscious. This particular autosuggestion ought to become part of their lives, however, any other autosuggestion can be repeated at anytime, anywhere, for example before the start of tests at school they can repeat the following sentence: "I am going to pass this test. I am going to pass this test. I am going to pass this test". Etc. etc. … and they will pass the test!

Dear Parents, as a last thought, always remember:

With patience and perseverance, the spoken word is mightier than the cane.

VISUALISATION

The powers of the human mind are truly remarkable. Among all these great powers, mental vision is one of the greatest. Just imagine being able to visualise in your mind some way-out event or invention, repeat your visualisation often over time until it is impressed in your unconscious, then focus on it or just store it until, at the appropriate time (sometimes unexpected!), the way-out dream becomes reality.

Some of the most successful people on our planet have achieved their goals with the help of their mental vision. From a young age they had dreams of becoming successful, be it in competitive sport or politics, as an actor, business-man or just plain and modest, by creating a healthy and happy family.

The ordinary person who hasn't focused yet on any particular goal in life is now able to do so by using the technic of visualisation, the artificial stimulation of the powers of imagination in the pursuit of a desired objective or goal.

Every day, in a relaxed state, spend some time visualising the reality you want. Picture yourself to be doing the thing you want to do or to be the person you want to be. Do not waste time lingering on visions of a future that is logically impossible or a future that might or could happen. Visualise your objective or goal in all its details, as if it was happening right now. Any doubts about future success are only natural. Try to ignore any doubts that may arise. Do not use the "effort of will" to fight them. Never let the imagination run amok, be precise, level headed and rational. Once you have settled down in your mental quest, start to focus on practicalities, educate yourself; if your goal lies in competitive sport, engage the services of a professional coach etc., etc. It may take some time but with patient determination carry on your quest for success. Do not let obstacles get in your way, however, if they do, remove them, one by one.

The most wonderful quality about visualisation is that once your mental vision is deeply impressed in your unconscious, it will simply guide you to your goal.

In the pursuit of creating a better world, we have to adhere to the following rules:

1. Do not waste your precious time visualising the impossible, ridiculous or downright bad.
2. The vision, your goal or objective must not have a detrimental effect on yourself, your family, society, nature or our planet, on the contrary, it ought to make a positive contribution to all of the above.

Any image held in your mind has the potential to become reality. Channel the power of your imagination in the right direction and you will find real meaning in life.

7

DEATH

THE END

Death is the termination of life. Normally, in humans or animals, death occurs at a mature stage of life with the gradual decline of metabolic processes followed by the complete failure of some vital organ or gland. Accidental death usually results from a combination of organic damage and shock.

Human beings fear death, the great leap into the dark, the unknown, the looming nothingness and/or the uncertainty surrounding the belief of an afterlife. It is not surprising that they dread its approach, especially if it implies to be an end filled with physical pain. But unlike other threats, this one can never be avoided, not in the least, not even if one were given all the powers of nature or medical prowess. Its approach is as certain as the changing of the seasons, as inevitable as night follows day, even more so -, and to add to is terror, death is immense, the ultimate victor, infinite in every way possible. It presents itself to the mind as the most total certainty, its immensity defies description.

What causes the emotions of fear, anxiety, sombreness, melancholy, helplessness, dejection and despondency? Is it the looming loss of one's possessions, of all that one has been working for throughout life; or is it the feeling at the end of one's life that all the hard work, the virtuous life and good deeds were not worth the effort; or the nagging doubt that the glorified afterlife may not turn out as promised; or the fear of future hell and damnation; or the feeling of not having achieved fulfilment, one's aspirations and dreams and the realization that it is too late now?

Yes, any of these reasons may greatly contribute to the normal sadness and lingering fear, provided of course that he or she has not succumbed to the artificially induced peace and tranquillity rendered by drugs or a natural progression of insanity. However, unless you are one of the many super-successfully indoctrinated followers of a religion, firmly convinced you will end up in heaven or find eternal peace in Nirvana, it may well be the thought of the annihilation of "self" and the stark, clear vision of final departure to nothingness that causes the main-thrust of negative emotions.

But what is "self", also known as the ego or "I"? Does it actually exist?

Carl Gustav Jung, the well-known Swiss psychologist describes the ego as the subject of one's consciousness and the self as the subject of one's totality.

Sigmund Freud divided the personality into three parts: the super ego, the ID and the ego. The superego represents the moral, social, prohibiting and censoring elements of the personality, it demands acceptable conduct. The ID is the primitive, biological and aggressive part of the personality, it drives for satisfaction. The ego, the self-asserting and self-preserving tendency, establishes a relationship with the environment on a reality principle. In a well-adjusted person, the ego acts as moderator between the super ego and the ID.

In its general sense, ego has the meaning of self and in scholastic philosophy it is defined as the entire person, body and mind considered as one.

After careful analysis backed by scientific studies, one probably finds that the self may be nothing more than a model of one's inner complex being, an un-cohesive mental image of a human-being riddled with contradictions, or – whatever else we may think or believe is the essence of our being. Many people are convinced that the self inside each of us exists only in the sense that we undeniably feel like individuals, distinct and different from our fellow human beings. Needless to say that the self, whatever our ideas are, will disappear into nothing with the death of our body. Anyway, where was the self before we were born? Where was anybody before planet earth came into being? As, Lucretius, one of the great Roman poets and philosophers once said: "the eternity after death is the mirror image of the eternity before birth".

Does such "realisation" eliminate the main thrust of negative emotions? No, it can still leave a soulless vacuum, an emotional emptiness, sadness and lingering fear of the unknown.

Dr Elisabeth Kübler-Ross, a Swiss authority and author of a well-known book on death and dying recognised five main stages of dying:

The first is conscious or subconscious denial and isolation.

The second is anger with themselves or directed at others, especially those close to them.

The third is bargaining with whatever God the person believes in (it rarely provides a sustainable solution).

The fourth is depression. It is a sort of acceptance with emotional attachment or a partial acceptance of reality.

The last stage is final acceptance. This varies greatly depending on the person's situation and mental state.

In reality, the experience of these five stages of dying may differ profoundly from person to person. Many may not even pass through some of the stages whilst other's sequence may differ greatly, however, it is final acceptance that raises an important question. Could something else deep inside all of us, an animating principle or everlasting soul, more spiritual, divine and superior in nature than the ego or self could ever be, open the portals to eternal life?

Anyway, how do we explain the millions of faithful who unquestionably believe in an after-life?

Surely these people, most of them reasonably sound in body and mind, cannot all be wrong, or can they?

AFTER-LIFE

THE PERSUASION OF THE TRUTH

Ever since gaining self-awareness, homo-sapiens must have felt strongly that there is more to death than just an abrupt termination of one's life. Among early human ancestry the desire for boundless existence was so profound that they contrived diverse conjectures of after-life suitable to their way of life. Evidence for ritual burials date back as far as the times of the Neanderthal man. Sigmund Freud called the desire for an afterlife

"The oldest, strongest and most insistent wish of mankind".

Possibly the main reason why the after-life was so prominent in human speculation was the fact that the after-life links up with the fundamental problem of human existence and purpose on earth. People throughout history, from all walks of life all around the world ask themselves the same pertinent questions: "what is the purpose of living a virtuous life if there is no reward forthcoming in the after-life"? "Why shouldn't a high living, successful criminal be punished in an after-life if justice did not prevail in this life"? "What is the purpose in just being born to exist and then die"? etc. etc. . . . . .

The majority of the world's religions believe in the immortality of the soul but there are divided opinions among them over the future state of the soul and over its activities in eternity.

What is the soul?

The term originates from the old English "Sāwol" (German: Seele). It is a kind of unification term that, at all levels of social development, denotes the non-material, spiritual and animating principle of life. As a consequence of its status it also signifies the human element that survives death. Over the course of history, philosophers and academics also used the terms "self", mind, spirit and psyche as the equivalent of soul either intentional or because of lack of knowledge.

Evidence of a belief in the existence of a soul dates back to Neolithic times. Among primitive cultures, the soul was not to have an existence independent of the body it animated. It was conceived to be a shadow in and around the body, invisible but manifest in much the same way breath is invisible but manifest.

The great pyramid of Cheops in Egypt was built in 2720 B.C., a lasting monument to the early belief in an after-life. The early Egyptians gave the soul immortality but materialized it by giving it bodily needs. They took elaborate care to preserve the body, convinced that at some future time the body would be united with the soul (or souls) lingering there.

The basic texts of Hindu philosophy and theology, the Upanishads, were compiled between 800 and 500 BC. They were the works of many authors and consisted of more than 100 discourses, a collection of ideas on the nature of things and their relationship to the universe. What I find remarkable is that they conceived the soul as a manifestation of the supreme being, the life giving principle and as such it was part of all forms of life, be it plants, animals or humans.

Among some of the early Greek philosophers the nature of soul was sought in matter. Anaximenes was of the opinion that it was air. Heraclitus, "the weeping philosopher", born 540 B.C., thought it was fire. Democritus, "the laughing philosopher", born between 470 and 460 B.C., was convinced it was the finest of the atoms.

Pythagoras, the celebrated Greek philosopher and mathematician, born about 582 B.C., conceived the soul as the sum of all the parts of the body. A properly balanced body will carry a harmonious immortal soul which is passed after death successively into other bodies (metempsychosis).

Socrates, born near Athens about 469 B.C., was the first philosopher to teach that the individual human soul is a miniature of the soul of the universe and the seat of good and evil. He views knowledge as good because it results in virtue which is the highest end in life. Evil results from ignorance which arises when the soul is ruled by the body. Thus the soul, eternal in nature and striving to re-unite with the universal soul, became the centre of ethical behaviour.

Plato (427 – 347 B.C.), a pupil of Socrates, transmitted and amplified his teacher's ideas. After Socrates's premature death in 399 B.C., Plato went on to develop the concept of soul to that of a prime mover of life. As a consequence all ethical qualities, good and bad, have their origin in the soul.

Aristotle (384 – 322 B.C.) was a disciple of Plato. However, he did not consider the soul to be immortal but conceived it to be an entity similar to the body located inside the heart (the brain was thought to be filled with phlegm, and considered to be acting as a cooling system). He believed the soul was the vital principle of life, its spiritual essence giving the organisms permeated by it the qualities of living things. Aristotle taught the existence of three levels of soul: The vegetable, which performed the functions of growth and reproduction, the animal, which contained the power of locomotion and sensation and the rational which was found only in human beings. The heart remained the seat of the soul until about 160 A.D.

Galen (130 – 200 A.D.), a celebrated Greek physician was first in pointing to the brain as the site of mental activity and Aristotle's three levels of soul. Later, he also added memory and imagination to those three basic elements. Galen became the dominant authority in the fields of medicine, physiology, philosophy of logic and religion. He died in Sicily about 200 A.D. The influence of his work was so great that even the all-powerful Roman Catholic church, after reinstating the immortality of the soul, appropriated most of Galen's findings. The wide acceptance of his ideas extended until the 16th century. With the renaissance came a general re-awakening of the spirit of enquiry.

René Descartes (1596 – 1650), a French philosopher and mathematician distinguished himself as a leading proponent of independent thought. He had very definite views on the nature of body, soul, matter and mind. Descartes believed himself to be a mental being, completely distinct from his body. "I think, therefore I am" were his memorable words. From the deep divide between the mental and the physical aspects of a human being, he inferred that mind ought to be able to continue to exist after the death of his body. This, he thought, was proof that every human possesses an immortal soul.

The English philosopher Thomas Hobbes (1588 – 1679) was deeply influenced by the scientists of the day, in particular Galilei Galileo, a distinguished Italian physicist who made a series of most important astronomical discoveries. Hobbes's views on the subject of soul were profoundly mechanical. The brain, alias mind, alias soul is nothing more than a thinking machine, he says. What he probably meant was the equivalent of a modern day computer, to be discarded after use.

Many more materialist philosophers followed in his wake and it was up to religion to keep the flag flying.

In pre-exilic Judaism the soul was conceived of in the manner of many primitive cultures. "And God breathed into his nostrils the breath of life, and man became a living soul" (Gen. 2:7). Thus reads a passage in the story of the creation. In post-exilic Judaism the belief slowly developed that the soul was eternal and was distinct from the body. This concept evolved into the Talmudic doctrine that the soul was the seat of virtue and that evil stemmed from the lusts of the flesh.

In Christianity, Jesus instilled a deep consciousness of the individual soul by making its salvation or damnation the supreme question for every human being. Christians believe that the soul is pure spirit, immortal and created by God. They regard it as the fountain head of reason but also as the source of love and sympathy. Relative to salvation or damnation, most Christians admit the soul's responsibility to God for the deeds done during one's lifetime. However, some churches adhere to a doctrine of predestination, believing that the destiny of every soul was fixed by an omnipotent and omniscient God at the creation. The orthodox view contends that at the final judgement, the lot of every soul will be irrevocably fixed.

The Mohammedan religion has similar views to Christianity. The Koran, the holy book of the Muslim world clearly states that the gates of heaven shall not be open to sinners and unbelievers. For them, hell is their reward but the believer and the righteous will be "companions of the garden for ever".

The Buddhists believe that there is no ego, soul or anything substantial or lasting, but all things are subject to change, not remaining the same for two consecutive moments. There is continuity but no identity. All things are impermanent, an arising and a ceasing of things. Nothing is lasting. Buddhism is not a one-life-after-death theory. It supports a chain of existence, repeated existence. The Buddhist theory of re-birth has its origin in the enlightenment of the Buddha. Rebirth is the nearest and least objectionable term, but it is not something permanent that after death takes flesh again. It is more like renewed existence. Kamma is the law of moral causation that shapes the destiny of beings and brings about rebirth. Kamma is perfect justice, each one becomes what one deserves. A dying man can be reborn in states that are non-human, depending on his kamma, or good and evil actions. Is there an end to this repeated existence? Yes, the seeker for deliverance practices the noble eightfold path (avoiding extremes!) that leads to enlightenment and final deliverance.

So many ideas, opinion and beliefs; so many dogmas, tenets and doctrines, so many truths . . . . . .

Unfortunately for humankind, nobody ever has come back again from "the beyond" to tell us what to believe and what not to believe. Death really seems like a black hole, an abyss with no possibility of return . . . . . .

or is there?

Spiritualism refers to the belief that the souls of the dead retain the personalities they had in life and that, through the services of a living human being, commonly known as a medium, they can communicate with the living. Although the belief that the dead are able to manifest themselves has existed from time immemorial, spiritualism as an organised movement has existed only since 1848. It all started in a village called Hydesville, New York. When John D. Knox and his two young daughters began to hear strange knockings in their house they believed that some immortal soul was trying to contact them. Later they even translated the noise into a code for the purpose of communicating with the spirits. The natural human desire to communicate with persons departed caused the news of the Knox phenomena and later other claims and demonstrations, to spread like a wild fire. Hundreds of people streamed to séances organised by spiritualists. In 1852, the movement spread to England where the number of practising mediums and séances grew to impressive proportions. The backlash came toward the end of the 19th century with revelations of widespread fraud among its practitioners. Early investigations revealed that with few exceptions, most of them were professional illusionists duping or beguiling the public (and they still do!). Subsequent investigations, in particular those organised by reputable teams of para-psychologists, led to the conclusion that some of the mystery surrounding telepathy was the result of as yet little understood psychological factors in a few gifted people seemingly able to break through barriers of ordinary space and time. Perhaps another example of the great potential of the human mind! A word of warning though; con-men are masters in make-believe, preying on millions of gullible people in need of stimulating miracles to escape the hard, dry facts of everyday life. Make it a rule in life to question everything. The truth may hurt but it is preferable to letting your mind be ruled by falsehood or delusions.

NDE (NEAR-DEATH EXPERIENCE)

Many people have come very close to death or may have even been pronounced clinically dead but survived, either by good fortune, effective health care or both. Can these people offer us a glimpse of what to expect when our time comes? A large number, including some respected scientists, believe they can.

Individuals that were involved in accidents, attempted suicide or suffered massive heart attacks may have stopped breathing and been without a heartbeat for up to an hour and in extreme cases even longer, but unlike in the past, today's improved resuscitation techniques have vastly increased the chances of bringing people back from the twilight zone between life and death. Those that do survive a near-death experience at least give us an opportunity to study at first hand the boundaries between life and the looming darkness beyond.

Near-death experiences include anything from being woken up from a "peaceful sleep" in a mortuary (as happened to Ndoh Dlamini, a singer and performer from South Africa!) to most remarkable experiences such as floating above their body, traveling inside a tunnel towards a white light and encountering benign ghost -like figures resembling Jesus or some either deity. For most of those that have experienced the later, it was a most powerful and convincing testimony for the existence of an afterlife.

The research pioneers of NDE were Raymond Moody, a psychiatrist from Georgia, U.S.A.; Ralph Noyes, a psychiatrist at the University College of Medicine of Iowa, U.S.A.; Kenneth Ring, a psychologist at the University of Connecticut, U.S.A. and Dr Elisabeth Kübler-Ross.

Kenneth Ring published a book in 1980 titled "Life at Death: A Scientific Investigation of the Near-Death Experiences" in which he compiled the result of his interviews with 102 people who came very close to death. Roughly fifty per cent of them had an NDE. From these he was able to distinguish a number of recurring themes which tended to follow in similar order. First and foremost on his list was "a feeling of peace" (60 per cent of those interviewed) followed by an "out-of-body sensation" (37 per cent), "travelling along a tunnel" (23 per cent), a "light at the end of the tunnel" (16 per cent), and lastly "an overall penetration of light" (10 per cent).

If you compare these results with the results of a gallap poll conducted in the U.S.A. in 1982, you will notice that the percentage figures are not in close agreement with Kenneth Ring's. However, the similarity of experiences is simply remarkable. According to the poll, five per cent of Americans had a near-death experience and approximately fifty per cent of those interviewed claimed to have had an NDE. For the purpose of covering a wide spectrum, the NDE was broken down into ten different themes with the following results (Ring's percentages in bracket):

Feeling of Peace and Serenity	32 per cent	(60 per cent)
Life Review	32 per cent	
Entering Another World	32 per cent	
Out of Body Sensation	26 per cent	(37 per cent)
Accurate Visual Perception	23 per cent	
Encountering Other Beings	23 per cent	
Audible Sounds of Voices	17 per cent	
Light	14 per cent	(16 per cent)
Tunnel	9 per cent	(23 per cent)
Subsequent incidences of precognition	6 per cent	
(Penetration of Light)		(10 per cent)

After further countless scientific investigations there can be no doubt in anybody's mind, NDE exists and is here to stay, an extraordinary phenomenon, complementary to "peaceful sleep" before actual death. It is understandable that most people, after being directly or indirectly involved in an NDE, believe that the experience is a prelude or at least a sign of what can be expected after death. As a consequence a majority of ex-NDE patients become more religious, less materialistic and show more compassion to the plight of others.

How can we explain an NDE?

Before we jump to conclusions and accept the experience to be proof of the existence of an afterlife, we have to ask ourselves: could this phenomenon, in spite of the profound impression it has on the person, not have a natural, logical explanation? Could it not be a powerful illusion, a hallucinatory projection of the dying brain?

I do not want to delve too deeply into the subject matter but I need to explain that many books about NDE, including best sellers, are full of unverified tales, remarkable claims impossible to confirm or deny and stories of so-called controlled procedures where upon investigation several loop-holes were found. However, extensive scientific research by neurologists, neurobiologists and psychologists relating to hallucinations and NDE has been conducted. Their conclusions were that most of those recurring visual and audible themes associated with NDE can be explained by way of processes that occur in the brain when senses disintegrate and memory (sometimes distorted) takes over. Similar images appear in hallucinations caused by LSD, combinations of prescription drugs and alcohol, psychic episodes, sensory and oxygen deprivation and many others.

Apart from the visual and audible aspects of NDE, the most striking and long lasting impressions are:

a)   Feelings of peace and serenity and
b)   a kind of "super- consciousness"

a)   The feeling of peace close to death is an almost universal phenomenon. In the normal process of dying it is part of the last stage, which, according to Dr Elisabeth Kübler-Ross, is "final acceptance". The recollections of most patients whose heart stopped beating after an accident or attempted suicide were extreme feelings of peace and quietude with no sensations of pain, fear or anguish. The probable reason for this exalted state is a kind of "shut-off mechanism" in humans and most likely in higher developed animals to prevent unnecessary pain near death. Pain is necessary during the normal course of one's life to tell the brain that something is wrong with the body and some kind of action has to be taken. However, an extreme overload of pain in a badly damaged body does not serve any purpose, on the contrary, it is extremely counter-productive if there is still a chance of recovery.

b) the other striking and in many instances life-transforming impression on the minds of many people who made the journey to death's door is a sudden expansion of consciousness, a **"super-nova of consciousness"**.

During the course of a near-death experience some patients unexpectedly experience "highly intensified cognition". Their minds suddenly flare into spectacular activity, possibly using seldom or never utilised parts of the brain (neuro-scientists tell us that during its lifetime only a small percentage of the human brain is fully utilized). During this "expansion of consciousness", the patient becomes less aware of himself and more conscious of everything else, in other words, his self-consciousness fades and his insight into things other than himself becomes profound, attaining an almost mystical quality.

What does it mean?

Is it a step back down the ladder of evolution or, as many of the converted try to make us believe, is it perhaps a foretaste of after-life or life beyond human existence?

I do not think so.

My conclusion is as follows: the "super-nova of consciousness" is nothing else but an "outburst of exalted surreal cognition" (fully enhanced by an air of mysticism) shortly before the mind enters death's door.

Knowing that some truths transcend rationality, I still strongly believe that at the present time of human development it is imperative that we continue to base truth, wherever possible, on logic and rational thinking. Human knowledge is still in the kindergarten stage and to deliberately push irrationality into the foreground is highly irresponsible. This is corroborated by the fact that (mentioned previously) so far nobody has **actually** come back from **factual** death to report back to us.

DELUSIONS

To believe is to regard as true.

How many different "truths" relating to the ideas of everlasting soul, self, ego, or NDE exist in the minds of human beings? Hundreds, thousands?

We do not know,

If you were born in Neolithic times of stone age parents, you may have believed that the soul was part of you, invisible in and around the body.

If you were walking the streets around Ephesus, Asia Minor in 560 BC you may have been convinced by Heraclitus, the pessimistic philosopher, that fire was the soul and the beginning of all things.

If you were born in Thailand of Buddhist parents you may not know of the existence of a soul. Repeatedly told by your parents and teachers you may be convinced that after death you will be re-born into this world, transformed into something else depending on your present good or evil actions.

If you were born in Germany of Catholic parents you may believe that your soul is pure spirit and everlasting. Depending on your deeds during this lifetime, at the final judgement it may end up in heaven or hell . . . . and so it continues, truth after truth. Shot-Pot-Luck, a different geographic region or born in a different time may have decided which truth you believe.

Does it actually matter what we believe as long as it makes us happy, content and a better person because "the real truth" will never be known anyway?

One could take this light-hearted attitude and live happily ever after but human thirst for knowledge and wisdom cannot be stifled and I sincerely think that one day, after unceasing, painstaking separation of fancy from facts we will close in on some kind of truth that we can all agree on. Eventually, the word "soul" may fall by the wayside but the idea of an animating principle deserves to be taken seriously not only because it is deep-rooted in human speculation but it points to the crux question of our being: how did life originate?.

Throughout human history, people have believed in most extraordinary, stupendously silly and totally irrational ideas. Why? We cannot entirely blame human gullibility because it is not only the ignorant masses who succumb to the "spoken word" but under certain circumstances most of us would have fallen victim to, in my mind, unreasonable religious or philosophical "enlightenment". I want to mention one of the most extreme examples of religious intolerance: the inquisition of the Roman Catholic church. Just imagine living in Italy or Spain during the later years of the fifteenth century. A belief or knowledge contrary to the authorised teachings of the Roman Catholic church could have landed you alive on top of a pile of wood, surrounded by a crowd of spectators, condemned to be burned to death.

Heresy or any deviation from the accepted teachings or rites of the all-powerful church was punishable by horrendous physical and mental torture and death. Similar but less extreme examples of intolerance during the middle ages occurred in South America and the middle east. "The Good Word" was spread and consolidated successfully by means of an orgy of intolerance, spilt blood and threats of hell and damnation. Softer versions of religious intolerance still prevail but the basic means of spreading and consolidating "The Truth" have moderated in more recent times, however, a child brought up in a cohesive religious culture has little chance to escape never- ending indoctrination by parents, relatives, religious teachers, friends and congregation. As I have stated under the title "Suggestion – Autosuggestion in Parenthood", a child is very sensitive to suggestion, it tends to believe whatever its parents and teachers tell, often with slavish – naive gullibility, and with never ending repetitions year in and year out, the results are deeply, very deeply etched in the child's unconscious. For example cases exist where an adult person with similar childhood was persuaded and finally converted to a modern eastern-spiritual way of thinking but with approaching old age reverted back to the religion of its childhood. Such is the pull of early childhood indoctrination. Religious teachers know of the vulnerability of the child brain and the importance of early indoctrination. For this reason many churches have established youth education, holiday and entertainment centres to "keep their flock out of harm's way", especially during the very critical stage of adolescence. In more recent times many evangelical churches have complemented the conventional spreading and consolidation of "their truth" by performing so-called miracles of healing and the inducement of hypnoidal or ecstatic states (which often result in the participant's temporary physical collapse which they regard as spiritual or divine mediation).

Religion's power to comfort and console the dying, bereaved and lonely does not make it true. Whatever you believe, whatever church you may belong to, delusion is your constant companion; delusion surrounds you and sticks to you but it may also bring you happiness, comfort and satisfaction. You may think truth is not as important as human feelings, and as a believer in a good life after death you could never be disillusioned anyway. However, there may still be a nagging doubt in your mind that life after death may not turn out to be so good – it may be different, shockingly different to your belief. Yes, like an invisible cloak around your shoulder, delusion is your constant companion. Wouldn't it be nice to know the truth, the real truth? It may hurt but it is the only thing that may set you free – in more ways than you think . . . .

THE TRUTH

Yes, well, at the very least it is my truth, free of fantasy and delusion but deep inside I dearly wish I could share it with you.

The hard, painful truth we must come to terms with is that we are not alive again after death; no ego, I, or self will survive. Being dead is no different to not yet being born. Only our image, words and deeds survive in the minds of those we leave behind, and our accomplishments, however small, serve as temporary monuments in an ever-changing world.

Sometimes we consider nature to be beautiful, kind, soft, warm and full of love. During moments like these we simply forget the other side, the merciless cruelty of nature when for example a raging lion kills a delicate and innocent looking young antelope, or a poor and innocent child lies down on the sandy floor in the Sahara desert, ready to die of starvation.

But the cruelty is human perception. In reality, nature is neither cruel nor kind. It only does what it is programmed to do, and we all are part of nature. The fact that we are, as spearhead of evolution, equipped with a superior brain does not make any difference. When death knocks on our door, no mind-created fantasy can save us from the inevitable end.

We do not fear losing consciousness as long as we are reasonably assured of waking up again, but everlasting sleep, peace and quietness we fear and this is only natural but does this fear give us the right to fabricate doctrines of after-life? Do we really want to find solace by deluding ourselves? Surely, the answer is NO.

Now just consider the following: with what quality of mind (a normal self-conscious mind separates humans from lower forms of life) does a person suffering from irreversible brain damage, schizophrenia or any other serious mental disorder enter the kingdom of death? Certainly very poor and probably poorer than any animal mind. Even a mentally retarded child will never fully understand the real meaning of death or deceptive promises of an afterlife. Through unfortunate circumstances, these people are freed of delusions of life after death, good or bad. Their badly damaged or malfunctioning brain does not allow them to execute normal processes of thought.

Everybody can be free (or freed) of mental garbage without the experience of a badly damaged brain but it can only happen if one applies rational thought and questions everything society suggests or imposes on you. People already infected with the virus of deception ought to use any means possible, including long periods of auto-suggestion, to rid themselves of the disease. It is statistically unproven but nevertheless said that people who believe in an afterlife are more afraid of death than people who are free of such convictions. But let us be honest, most humans dread its approach. If you feel you can face the hard truth unaided, well, go ahead. However, if you think you will be in need of mental and emotional support when death finally knocks on your door, subscribe to a program of mental preparation. Ideally, this ought to be done long before the approach of old age as the implementation of this program constitutes an important step up the ladder of your personal development.

The first step is to let go, loosen your mental grip on material possessions. Too many possessions clutter life and the mind. Do not accumulate material riches as boost to the ego or props to a position in society. Cultivate an attitude of non-attachment or inward poverty. It ensures that all outer wealth is used without the user being enslaved by it. Regard your possessions not as personal property but as things on loan, entrusted to you to be revoked at any moment. Dissolution is a fact of life. The concept of property can also be applied to people. Do not regard your children, husband or wife as if they were your possessions to be controlled at will. No person has any right to power over another, neither in its destiny nor its affections. Love and friendship ought to be undemanding and un-possessive. Give affections rather than seek for affection.

The second step is to acquire peace of mind. Most of your life is spent thinking and contemplating unimportant and irrelevant trivialities, scraps of remembered conversation, mulling over bits of gossip or unnecessarily worrying about your health and finances, what friends may think of you etc. etc. Most of these thoughts serve no practical purpose, on the contrary, they may lead to states of chronic anxiety, bad health and depression. Unnecessary concern about events in the future is particularly wasteful of energy. Rather spend time with constructive and creative planning for the future. A muddled mind is fertile ground for the planting of delusions, deceits and fantasies, yet, one clings tenaciously to these wasteful thought processes, ignorant of the fact that peace of mind leads to more appropriate and purposeful actions.

The general control of mind is a slow process, requiring repeated practice and **constant awareness.**

Become aware of your wasteful habits and uncontrolled, irrelevant thoughts. Cut them short immediately. Do this over and over again, never give up, even under trying, difficult conditions. In the beginning it is enough simply to try to remember that you have forgotten to be aware, then become aware of your daily, mostly mechanical activities from dressing yourself to walking down the street. Later try to be fully aware of yourself, your thoughts and your actions in all your activities.

Peace of mind can also be achieved by cultivating a more balanced outlook on life and an attitude of neutrality toward all pairs of opposites such as pleasure and pain, joy and sorrow, praise and blame, heat and cold and so forth. Do not excessively strive for fame and fortune, pleasure and gratification, over-exert yourself trying to achieve the impossible nor worry yourself sick if things do not turn out the way they should. The attitude of neutrality means that there should be no feeling of attraction for the one and aversion from the other. Naturally such feelings will continue to arise **but the intensity with which you react to them can be gradually reduced.**

The more deeply you become aware that all life is a continual interplay of opposing and complementary forces, the more easily can you maintain an attitude of acceptance in the face of its vicissitudes. This is not to say that you should not tend towards the good or away from the bad, but your striving should not be based on the illusion that we can have one without the other. The wise course is to seek between opposite extremes the transcending factor that reconciles them at a higher level: balance and moderation. Enjoy your pleasures and accept your sufferings but cling to neither. Both are inevitable but both will pass.

To secure peace of mind you have to reduce its agitation, meaning you should master negative feelings which drain energy and distort your view of life. Most of them are without basis in reality, discordant jangles in the natural harmony of things. At first it is sufficient to aim at being aware of these negative emotions, acknowledge them and recognise them for what they are.

Later, when you are able to become aware of them immediately they arise, you should try consciously to replace them by their opposite. Initiate a feeling of love or friendship in place of dislike; compassion for the suffering instead of indifference and sympathetic joy for the happy and fortunate instead of envy. Concerning yourself you may substitute faith for fear, patience for irritation but under no circumstances suppress negative emotions in which you pretend to yourself that you do not have them and merely drive them into the subconscious from where they eventually find expression in some other form. Where the conscious effort is insufficient to neutralize a negative feeling such as anger it is better that you should express it, however much your image of yourself may suffer as a result. Far better to lose your temper than seethe with resentment.

The following are perhaps the greatest aids for the attainment of fulfilment and subsequent peace of mind:

Appreciate the order of the universe.

Carry the torch of consciousness to ever greater heights.

Accept and comply with the ethical principle of universal validity.

With all the love and consideration you have for anything, your family deserves the most.

Whatever work you do, do it to the best of your ability.

Try to be humble.

Engage in physical exercise.

Cultivate a profound love for nature.

Peace of mind improves the quality of life and during the days and months before death, peace of mind is invaluable in order to facilitate the transition from life to death.

If the last days or months of your life are spent suffering physical pain, try your best to alleviate it by any means possible. When heavy doses of medication do not help or the state of your health has deteriorated beyond relief do not shy away from seeking help in enlightened places like Switzerland, the Netherlands or Oregon where euthanasia is legalised. It is extremely cruel to prolong the suffering of a person with no hope of relief.

If your life is well lived it is only natural to be sad on the eve of your departure, but nothing lasts forever, not even happiness! Days or months before death knocks on your door, try to gather your senses. Instead of wallowing in sadness or depression try to find yourself at one with nature; look outside your window or even better, go outside your house into the open-air. With clouds drifting across a clear-blue sky and the warming rays of the sun touching your face, be or imagine yourself to be among the flowers, trees, the birds and the bees and rejoice, you are part of nature; we all are, you and me and everybody else, alive or dead. Realise that nothing in this world is permanent or static, everything is subject to change and so are we, one day we are here, another day we are gone. Change or impermanence is the essential characteristic of all that exists in the physical world. All Is fleeting: the flower's beauty, the bird's melody, the bee's hum and a sunset's glory. Not a single atom that is in your body now was there when you were a child and wherever you look there is a never-ending exchange of particles, a transfer of energy from being to being, alive or dead. With your ego and your mind slowly drifting into nowhere, only the particles you are made of together with their energy tied to Potentia will survive and none of this energy will ever get lost.

NEVER EVER.

ELEMENTS OF YOU ARE PART OF THE UNIVERSE **FOR EVER**.

Printed in the United States
By Bookmasters